HIDDEN
HISTORY
of
EAST MEADOW

HIDDEN
HISTORY
of
EAST MEADOW

Dr. Scott M. Eckers

THE
History
PRESS

Published by The History Press
Charleston, SC
www.historypress.com

Images are from the author's collection unless otherwise noted.

First published 2022

Manufactured in the United States

ISBN 9781467149624

Library of Congress Control Number: 2022939482

Notice: The information in this book is true and complete to the best of our knowledge. It is offered without guarantee on the part of the author or The History Press. The author and The History Press disclaim all liability in connection with the use of this book.

For Jenny and Jacob.

This work is a follow-up to East Meadow *(2016)
in Arcadia Publishing's Images of America series.*

Please visit www.eastmeadowhistory.org, the companion website to both books.

East Meadow High School Marching Band on Hempstead Turnpike. *Bill Katz.*

Contents

CONTENTS

Part I
FARMS AND ESTATES

The Winter Gardens, Brookholt, Hempstead, N. Y.

Winter Gardens at Brookholt, north of Front Street. *Art Kleiner.*

EARLY SETTLEMENTS AND OUR HAMLET'S NAME

East Meadow is an unincorporated hamlet within Nassau County's town of Hempstead. This means that it does not have its own governing body like a village or city and is a "census-designated place" by virtue of having institutions named "East Meadow" by which its residents identify. These include the school district, a post office, a fire department and names of businesses. There is no "establishment" date of East Meadow because it has never been incorporated. The use of the name goes back hundreds of years—not long after the establishment of Hempstead Town in 1644.

Before the arrival of the Europeans, the earliest residents of the Hempstead Plains were tribes of Algonquian Indians. The name Merrick (alternatively spelled "Meroke," "Merioke" and "Mericock") stems from a reference to the plains themselves. In the Massachusetts language, the term means "bare land." The land was certainly bare! The East Meadow area was almost completely devoid of trees; some of our oldest trees were imported from places as far as England. The land was covered with brush, however, which led some early settlers to call the place Brushy Plains.

In November 1643, the land now encompassing East Meadow was sold to Englishmen John Carman and Robert Fordham by members of the local Massapequa, Merrick and Rockaway tribes. Carman and Fordham had arrived in the Dutch colony from Connecticut and obtained permission from Dutch Director-General William Kieft to purchase the land from these Algonquian peoples. During the British colonial period, Hempstead Town was part of one of the original New York counties: Queens. (It was not until after the 1898 incorporation of western Queens County into Greater New York City that Nassau County was born.) "Hempstead" is likely a variation of a word for "town-spot," suggesting its central importance as a settlement in Queens. Both English and Dutch settlers lived on Long Island. The "East Meadow" of the Hempstead village was convenient for grazing, and town residents held the area in common for their cattle, sheep and other livestock. The earliest recorded use of the name appeared in town records in 1658. William Jacocks and Edward Raynor were authorized to keep cows in "the East Meadow" from spring to fall.

During the American Revolution, the British held New York City and much of Long Island for the entire war. Local residents' loyalties were divided, although some men took up the cause of independence. Hempstead Town's Richard Gildersleeve, for instance, signed a declaration on July 19, 1776, promising to "obey the orders of the Provincial and Continental Congress in defense of liberty, never to fight against the Americans or help the British." Those residing in the southern parts of Hempstead were generally Loyalists, supporting the British Crown; those residing in the northern parts of the town were generally Patriots, heralding the cause for independence. This rift was so significant that the town split after the war ended. In 1784, North Hempstead Town was established by its proud Patriots. The non-seceding southern part, with its "East Meadow," was known as South Hempstead before reverting to Hempstead in 1796. The federal census of 1790 clearly enumerates the population of the township of South Hempstead (3,826 people, including 326 slaves), but the 1800 federal census lists 4,141 people in the town of Hempstead, with a note that it is synonymous with South Hempstead.

Rural Life in the Nineteenth Century

The 1850 federal census was the first to collect detailed information on each person living in a household (and not just the head of that house), including, for the first time, local "civil divisions." Therefore, the difficulty of genealogical research in hamlets such as East Meadow increases prior to 1850.

In 1821, Samuel Carman, Benjamin Spragg and Robert Van De Waters raised $10,000 and incorporated the East Meadow Canal Company. The idea was to build a canal through the "East Meadow Swamp" in order to bring water from the Hempstead (East) Bay via Merrick to East Meadow and the Hempstead Plains. The city of Brooklyn was growing exponentially in the mid-nineteenth century and was thirsty for water. In March 1854, Brooklyn's Water Committee presented a plan that would create a series of canals and conduits to bring fresh water from rural Long Island streams to the city's residents. One of those waterways was the East Meadow Brook (or Creek), which was expected to provide 7 million of 32.5 million total gallons of water each day. Water in the creek, which ran south toward Merrick, was relatively pure at two grains of impurities per gallon. Brooklyn moved forward with its plan, purchased ponds and lands near the future South Side Railroad of Long Island paralleling today's Sunrise Highway and built conduits through Queens and Kings Counties (hence the names Conduit and Force Tube Avenues). The city completed the initial project in 1862 but did not utilize the East Meadow Brook until 1889, when it built pipes as far as Massapequa. When the city of Brooklyn consolidated with New York City in 1898, the supply became the New York City Water Works. Not all residents were thrilled with the plan, and some believed that the waters would run dry. Freeport residents unsuccessfully sued the company in 1904 for damage to their oyster businesses. It was not until the 1953 extension of the Meadowbrook Parkway, however, that the East Meadow Brook was seriously threatened. In the East Meadow area, the brook remains a shadow of its former self and is dry in many places. Farther south, the brook still runs into ponds.

Life in East Meadow before the Civil War was based almost entirely on farming. News of the antebellum period often highlighted the local misfortunes that occasionally plagued agrarian life: barn fires, thefts, mischief and curiosities such as the white wild geese flock that landed in 1833. Marriages were celebrated of men and women who found partners quite locally. Only a handful of surnames were common in town, many tracing back to the earliest European settlers in Hempstead. By midcentury, the hamlet was not immune to the greater threat tearing apart the nation, however, and bravely sent sons into battle. The 1863 draft, which prompted bloody riots in the streets of New York and other cities, affected those living in the countryside as well. Twenty-five East Meadow residents were conscripted into military service:

NAME	AGE	OCCUPATION	RESIDENCE
Buckhardt, Conrad	35	Farmer	East Meadow
Carman, Charles	29	Farmer	East Meadow
Carman, Cornelius	41	Blacksmith	East Meadow
Cass, Samuel	44	Laborer	East Meadow
Cheshire, Towsend	40	Laborer	East Meadow
Daffer, John	42	Laborer	East Meadow
Denton, Lewis, Jr.	20	Laborer	East Meadow
Denton, William	23	Laborer	East Meadow
Doty, David	20	Laborer	East Meadow
Duryea, Andrew	44	Farmer	East Meadow
Fish, Elbert R.	22	Farmer	East Meadow
Lewis, Peter	24	Paper Maker	East Meadow
Lewis, William	28	Laborer	East Meadow
McKillan, Joseph	32	Laborer	East Meadow
Post, Samuel	26	Hay Carter	East Meadow
Seaman, John	23	Laborer	East Meadow
Seaman, William	30	Innkeeper	East Meadow
Skillicam, John	24	Laborer	East Meadow
Smith, Henry	37	Farmer	East Meadow
Smith, John	23	Laborer	East Meadow
Smith, Moses	20	Laborer	East Meadow
Sprague, Elbert	20	Laborer	East Meadow
Sprague, Seely	22	Farmer	East Meadow

NAME	AGE	OCCUPATION	RESIDENCE
Sprague, William	25	Farmer	East Meadow
Valentine, Daniel S.	35	Shoemaker	East Meadow
Van Nostrand, Wesley	35	Farmer	East Meadow
Baldwin, Abraham	26	Farmer	New Bridge
Baldwin, Bedell	21	Farmer	New Bridge
Bayman, Alfred	20	Bayman	New Bridge
Bayman, Moses	22	Bayman	New Bridge
Bedell, David	32	Farmer	New Bridge
Foote, Andrew S.	38	Schoolteacher	New Bridge
Seaman, Elbert W.	27	Farmer	New Bridge
Seaman, Henry	25	Farmer	New Bridge
Seaman, Thomas, Jr.	23	Farmer	New Bridge
Smith, Nelson H.	29	Merchant	New Bridge

The Civil War and Reconstruction period did not fundamentally alter agrarian life, and newspapers continued to report on farming matters. The 1863–64 season was bad for keeping cows, as at least three of the valuable animals wandered from home (those of Ezekiel Abrahams, Mary Noon and William Seaman), necessitating $5 rewards for their return! Samuel and Jeremiah Post's barn near Prospect Avenue burned down in 1864, but they were only insured for half the $400 loss. Hector Curtis's barn was burned down by children in 1865. In 1866, John Place's six fowls were stolen from his home near the current-day fire department headquarters. John Smith (who lived near current-day Prospect and Chambers Avenues) lost twenty. Sealey/Seeley Sprague's chickens and turkeys disappeared from his farm. Lott Carman lost thirty. Other big news included wedding announcements, farm foreclosures and real estate transactions. In 1882, pickles—yes, pickles—made the news when East Meadow farmers would not agree to the terms of the Pickle Company of Jerusalem's payment plan. The following year, a historic tornado leveled barns all over the community. In 1910, wild dogs were to blame for killing pets and chickens of Amos Rhodes, Elmer Stringham and George Littleton, all of whom worked the land near the corner of North Jerusalem Road and Bellmore Avenue. Rhodes had been arrested in 1890 for stealing a hive of bees.

Baseball was popular in the 1880s, and East Meadow had two clubs: Red Stars and Hempstead Blues.

East Meadow's popular name never changed but became known differently with changing times and shifting economies. The East Meadow, described in by Richard Bayles in 1885 as "smiling with abundant crops," was perfect for the farming period. When the Meadow Brook Club entertained the local high society members in the late nineteenth and early twentieth centuries (annual membership fees were $5,000 to $6,000!), residents used Meadow Brook or East Meadow Brook as a synonym for East Meadow (especially when referring to the western part of the hamlet near the Barnum property and the brook itself). The area near the intersection of current-day Newbridge Road and Old Westbury Road was a neighborhood called New Bridge. This designation was also used south toward North Jerusalem Road. Documents from as early as 1821 refer to the road as "New-Bridge Path." As the village of Hempstead grew in importance following World War I, East Meadow was often synonymous with East Hempstead (a description also used for Uniondale). The place names were used interchangeably, particularly when discussing the Hempstead Turnpike/Front Street area.

HEMPSTEAD-BETHPAGE TURNPIKE

Hempstead-Bethpage Turnpike started out as two turnpikes. In nineteenth-century America, roads were generally inadequate for long-distance travel. Early in the century, the National Road was built as a taxpayer-funded experiment, but canals and railroads were king when it came to 1800s infrastructure. The main roads constructed at that time were private (toll) turnpikes, built and maintained by corporations. Hempstead Turnpike was an early example and came about through New York State's passage of the Turnpike Acts of 1807. In 1812, the route was incorporated by Samuel Carman, Joseph Pettit, Abraham Bell and Laurence Seaman. The road followed old Native American trails, as did so many other routes in the New York region. The Hempstead Turnpike Company, as established in March 1812, was authorized to "run and operate a turnpike road from the Village of Jamaica to the Village of Hempstead in perpetuity." The collection of public town roads that made up the turnpike at its inception were turned over the company for improvement, widening and maintenance.

Similarly, Bethpage Turnpike Company was incorporated April 1829. Rulef Dureya, Richard Willets, Daniel Raider, John Powell, Albert Hentz and Benjamin Thompson were authorized to essentially extend Hempstead Turnpike (Fulton Street) from the Presbyterian burying ground east to Bethpage and beyond.

It was a long and arduous drive to the New York City area. Traveling to and from East Meadow in the early nineteenth century was dependent on private stagecoach lines going east. Timetables were published in local newspapers. Miller and Carman ran a stage line from their Long Island Hotel at 13 Old Fulton Street in the city of Brooklyn every Tuesday and Saturday in 1841 at 1:00 p.m. In 1842, Bedell's Stage ran every Tuesday and Saturday at 2:00 p.m.

In 1852, the stockholders of Hempstead Turnpike Company sold the road to the Hempstead and Jamaica Plank Road Company. Improvements would come through the setting of wooden planks over the dirt, as supported by New York State's Plank Road Act of 1847. Although rudimentary by today's standards, this "innovation" was popular before the Civil War and greatly improved transportation along the turnpike. The New York State legislature passed a law in April 1859 that authorized the company to collect higher fees as soon as planking was completed along the route. The law stated that "for each mile traveled by wagons, or otherwise, drawn by one horse, mule or ox, the sum of one and one quarter cent per mile, and for each additional horse, mule or ox, the sum of one and one-quarter cent per mile." It was common for turnpikes to collect tolls on animals and not people, as many people used

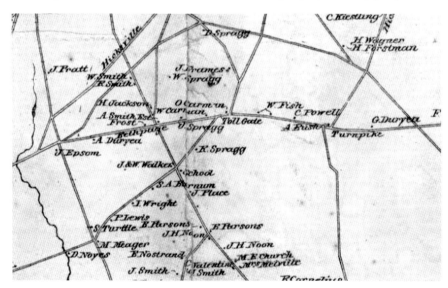

Bethpage Turnpike and vicinity, 1859. *Library of Congress.*

the roads to drive their livestock. The number of chickens, sheep or other animals one had with him determined the amount. The toll booth in East Meadow was run by the Carman family and was located on the north side of Hempstead-Bethpage Turnpike, just west of Carman Avenue.

In March 1882, the charter of the Hempstead and Jamaica Plank Road Company expired, and the original Hempstead Turnpike corporation met to try to reorganize. A lengthy court case ensued over its ownership; by 1891, the road seems to have been public once again. It was further modernized through macadamizing, which is the laying of crushed stone as pavement, and became a county road in 1896. Bethpage Turnpike Company surrendered its charter to the town in May 1888 and was incorporated into the county system in 1897, paving the way for an improved gravel roadbed. By the time the U.S. Highway System was established in the 1920s, public roads had become the norm. New York State incorporated Hempstead-Bethpage Turnpike as Route 24 into its new state highway system soon thereafter.

Common Lands No More: Stewart's Purchase

For about two hundred years, local farmers kept their livestock in the Common Lands of the Hempstead Plains, a tremendous area of native grasslands. The Plains stretched across the center of eastern Queens County, and the lands were owned by the Town of Hempstead for public use. The "common" lands were shared for grazing purposes in the East Meadow Hollow, through which the brook flowed. The first land division took place in 1647, three years after the town was established with all lands held in common. Sixty-six men received the first allotments, with further divisions of the remaining 6,213 acres authorized after 1723. Townsfolk did not rush to divide the land but rather advertised "privilege of Common" when selling farms as private property. From 1659 on, landowners on the edge of the Plains were required to keep gates and fences around the Common Lands in good shape and were rewarded with grazing privileges proportionate to the number of sections they maintained. A law that year stated that "all the fences of ye frontiere lotts that runne into ye fields, shall be substantially and sufficiently fenced" or fines would be imposed.

Each year, East Meadow farmers let their cattle and sheep roam freely within these fences until the last Monday in October. On Parting Day, as it would come to be known, farmers collected their animals for the winter. In colonial times, the town supported a "Cow-Keeper," paid in butter and money, to oversee the distribution based on officially recorded earmarks. The hamlet would prove essential to townsfolk because "the commodity and advantage of the Inhabitants greatly depends on having access to the Publick wattering-places at the East Meadow." Such a bold statement from 1761 Town of Hempstead records caused leaders to act, authorizing paid positions to protect grasslands and lay out public highways there, for "there is some probability of Incroachments being made by some persons for their private Interest in Stoping up and Imbarrising the water to the great Damage of the Publick."

In 1862, a state law permitted towns to sell their common lands, but Hempstead Town's settlers were unconvinced of the benefits. It was East Meadow's most well-known woman, Sarah Ann Barnum, who orchestrated the sale. Known as the "eighth [honorary] member" of the Queens County Board of Supervisors, her considerable political influence is notable. She was responsible for convincing settlers to approve the sale of the Hempstead Plains that would pave the way for considerable East Meadow, and Town of Hempstead, development in return for a large sum of public money for school and welfare purposes. The public needed to decide whether to sell the public lands to speculator Charles Harvey for $42 per acre or wealthy New York City businessman Alexander Turney Stewart for $55 per acre. The main difference, aside from a price difference of $97,500, was what each purchaser would do with the property once it was acquired.

Harvey, a Tarrytown native who billed himself as a patriot and grandchild of a Revolutionary hero, was to turn the lands into a tremendous "truck farm"—that is, a farm on which fruits and vegetables are grown for sale by truck to New York City. The Common Lands had never been used for growing food before, and the public was skeptical about the soil quality. He offered the Town of Hempstead forty-two dollars per acre. Posters were printed on June 26, 1869; 105 petitioners joined town officials in asking citizens to vote on the Harvey deal on July 17.

Meanwhile, Stewart offered fifty-five dollars per acre for the Common Lands. He vowed to "open [the lands], by constructing extensive public roads, laying out the lands in parcels for sale to actual settlers, and erecting attractive buildings and residences, so that they may speedily be covered by a population desirable as neighbors, taxpayers, and citizens." The *New York Times* expressed its support for Stewart by telling its readers that they should look forward to the Common Lands' "speedy transformation from an uninviting, uninhabited waste, into the site of a busy, thriving, and prosperous population." On July 17, 1869, the votes were cast at John Pettit's

Left: Alexander Turney Stewart. *New York Public Library.*

Right: James Clinch Smith. *Encyclopedia Titanica.*

house in the village of Hempstead. Ultimately, two-thirds of the votes cast in town supported the Stewart deal.

The following week, the *Times* again reported on the favorable outcome of the sale. Nevertheless, legal challenges ensued: Harvey was incensed that the town commissioners backed out of his "completed" deal after he had given a $25,000 down payment. The editors of the *Times* asked Harvey and other detractors to "retire in disgust" and let Stewart develop the property so that Hempstead Town's population could increase and taxes could decrease. Stewart eventually purchased an additional two thousand acres, making his total landholdings more than nine thousand acres. He hired John Kellum as architect and general manager of the Hempstead Plains and went to work building his flagship village, Garden City, and the Central Railroad of Long Island in 1871. Stations in East Meadow, known as Meadow Brook (alternatively, Salisbury Plains) and New Bridge, opened in August 1873. The Long Island Rail Road acquired his line in 1881, and East Meadow saw regular train service until 1939. The tracks east of Uniondale, which crossed over the Wantagh State Parkway at grade, were removed in 1953 after Levittown's completion. Stewart's eponymous avenue originally continued through current-day Eisenhower Park. Only a few acres remain of the Hempstead Plains, located in Eisenhower Park and on the Nassau Community College campus.

In 1901, Stewart heir James Clinch Smith built a home on Stewart lands on Merrick Avenue, within today's Eisenhower Park. Smith, whose family is the namesake of his native Smithtown, was a noted horseman and a member of "The 400" society set. Smith's sister Bessie married famous architect Stanford White. In 1906, while watching a musical in the open-air rooftop theater of his own Madison Square Garden, White was shot and killed by Harry Thaw, who had aggressively pursued, and married, pinup actress Evelyn Nesbit—White's former underage lover. James Smith was one of the last people to talk to Thaw before the very public murder and testified in the "Trial of the Century" in 1907, which ultimately remanded Thaw to an insane asylum. Smith perished on the *Titanic* in 1912, apparently after heroically making sure women and children were rescued first. His mansion burned around 1938.

The Spragues' Misfortune Leads to a Hanging

Sprague (or Spragg) was a prominent family name in East Meadow. Their ancestors were original Hempstead settlers. At 6:30 a.m. on January 25, 1884, a masked man entered the home of Sealey Sprague, who lived on a farm located behind the current East Meadow High School athletic fields. Sarah Sprague was knocked to the ground and robbed of thirty-eight dollars. She summoned help from her neighbors, Peter Pettit and his family, who found her husband badly injured on a barn floor. Sealey was struck in the head with a fishplate, a metal bar used to hold railroad tracks together, and suffered a serious fracture to his head. Physicians initially believed that Sprague would not survive, but he made a slow and steady recovery over many months.

The unknown assailant fled through snow to a store in Westbury. The storekeeper, already aware of the suspect's description, caught Charles Rugg and held him until police arrived. Rugg was scheduled to be taken by train to Hicksville for examination by a local official. Twenty men assembled in East Meadow and took an oath to capture Rugg from Hicksville. They planned to bring the man to nineteenth-century justice by dragging him behind a horse if they could not find a suitable tree. Hundreds of locals apparently supported the effort. The district attorney, upon the advice of a few sensible residents who felt that lynching a Black man would bring shame on the local populace, decided to change the January 29 venue to Long Island City. Rugg narrowly escaped vigilante justice.

The East Meadow investigation was instrumental in solving several high-profile cases in the nearby town of Oyster Bay. On November 17, 1883, Lydia Maybee and her daughter Ann were strangled and murdered while an unknown criminal stole a gold watch, gold chain, cameo breast pin and cash with a total value of $130. The husband, Garret, survived the assault. A few weeks later, Mr. and Mrs. James Townsend were found beaten in their Oyster Bay home. These crimes rocked the town, and police followed many leads, accusing men who were later exonerated. After the arrest in the Sprague assault, it became clear that Rugg was connected to the Maybee and Townsend cases. Around the same time, a pawn shop owner identified Rugg as the man who brought in Maybee's gold watch.

In February 1884, Rugg penned a jailhouse confession in which he admitted to the highly publicized crimes. The jury took only one hour to find him guilty of seven counts of murder, assault and theft. He was hanged on the morning of May 15, 1885, at the Queens County Jail, to quite a bit of fanfare among Sheriff Garrett Furman and his police acquaintances. Having recently converted to Catholicism, Rugg received spiritual guidance from Father Maguire and walked to the gallows to "meet his fate without exhibiting any feeling." The denizens of East Meadow breathed a collective sigh of relief and were free to continue their safe and simple farming lives. The Spragues had no children; Sealey lived until 1917 and Sarah until 1937. Family members claimed that in her ninety-four years, Sarah left Long Island but once. The Sprague home, which had reportedly stood for close to three hundred years, was moved when Salisbury (Eisenhower) Park was built and eventually deconstructed in 1953.

Top: Sealey Sprague. *Susan Barkman Mantovani.*

Bottom: Sarah Sprague. *Mantovani.*

A LOVE TRIANGLE AND ATTEMPTED MURDER

The section of East Meadow and North Bellmore near Sabia's Corner (North Jerusalem and Newbridge Roads) was known to nineteenth-century locals as Hogshead, a name little used and long forgotten. The neighborhood was not known for its sophistication. It gained a reputation for having poorly educated, opioid-addicted, unhealthy, unhappy alcoholic laborers living in embarrassing shanties and working for a few respectable farmers. Of course, this exposé in sensationalist newspaper *The Sun* unfairly painted locals as yokels who believed that Hempstead was the big city, but the fact that several high-profile crimes in the 1880s were connected to the neighborhood did not help its image. "Hogshead" was connected by Bellmore (or Brush) Road, to "The Brush," a community of emancipated slaves and their families. Charles Rugg, a resident of that section, was executed in 1885 upon conviction of murder after an assault on the north side of town. The Brower family provided much excitement a few years later.

For much of the nineteenth century, the Brower (or Brewer) family lived near the intersection of Newbridge and North Jerusalem Roads, with another farm a block away at Newbridge Avenue. Parmenus and Jane (Carman) Brower's son Lewis married Sarah Ann Raynor around 1848 and took over operation of the family property with his parents. Lewis struck up a romantic relationship with Mary Jane Baldwin, who had been married twice and was previously known as Mrs. Samuel Lewis and Mrs. David Waring. Mary Jane was a younger woman who lived about a mile away on Bellmore Road in North Bellmore, across from brother DeWitt Clinton Baldwin and her mother Charity Southard's family. She became known as Lewis's "morganatic wife" who seemingly had free use of his farm's bounties. As Lewis became increasingly enamored of Mary Jane, he moved livestock and household goods to her cottage, neglecting his sickly wife (with whom he had children and grandchildren).

Sarah Ann, sensing her husband's growing estrangement, told her friend and neighbor (Mary) Elizabeth Spates that she might be murdered one night, as she was always alone. Elizabeth's husband was U.S. Navy captain Richard Nelson Spates, an adventurous and heroic Civil War veteran. Unfortunately, Sarah Ann had good precognition.

In the early morning hours of Saturday, September 10, 1887, Sarah Ann was axed in the head and suffered grave injuries. Lewis claimed to have been in bed, awakened by his wife's cry. The community, knowing of the Brower-Baldwin affair, rendered swift moral judgment and failed to believe his story.

Lewis Brower and Mary Jane Baldwin were both arrested for the "braining" and held at the Jamaica Town Hall. Lewis said that he went a mile away to his grandson rather than going to Powers, his nearest neighbor, because he was frightened. Barney Powers, a respected farmer, said that he saw Lewis washing blood off the axe. He went to the house with three sons, armed and ready to defend their neighbors. When they arrived, a dreadful sight met them. After searching in vain for "thieves," Lewis claimed that $342 in cash had been stolen from the house. Furniture had been disturbed in a way that the Powers might believe that a burglar had searched for the money. Neighbors knew that Brower was in significant farm debt and wouldn't have that kind of money in the house. Mrs. Spates found the weapon the following day, which had been suspiciously cleaned. Baldwin had seemingly fled to the Bellmore train station but was located. Coroner Philip Cronin was waiting to see if Sarah succumbed from her injuries before questioning the accused. Medical and legal professionals believed that death was imminent.

After several comatose days, Sarah Ann awoke and recalled some of the incident. On the night of the crime, she had gone to bed with Lewis at 9:30 p.m. or 10:00 p.m. She gave a lengthy deathbed statement to authorities alleging that Mary Jane Baldwin likely struck her before alleging that Lewis tried to kill her. Even if she were not partially paralyzed, the statement needed to be oral, as Mrs. Brower was illiterate.

On December 29, a coroner's jury found evidence enough to move forward with the case. They believed that Brower was responsible for his wife's injuries and held Mrs. Baldwin as a witness. The trial for attempted murder was held in Freeport's Euterpean or Union Hall. Mary Jane Lewis testified that she had not seen Brower since December 7. John Brower, Lewis's grandson, thought his grandmother did not receive medical care in a timely fashion: Dr. William Rhame was not called until late Saturday morning, at which time Sarah Ann had no pulse. Two surgeons from Hempstead, Drs. Searing and Handford, attended to Sarah Ann that night, almost an entire day after the attack. Dr. Rhame testified that after seeing her the next day, he did not think she would recover. She had a compound compressed skull fracture. Other wounds on her body were not made by the same axe.

Sarah Ann said that Lewis refused to come to bed that night. She was afraid to say who hit her, for fear that it would happen again, but said, "Well, I think Jane Baldwin struck the blows and father looked on and let her." Sarah Ann's daughter-in-law claimed she saw an axe or iron bar at Mary Jane's house. The bar had been kept for self-defense since the 1885 Rugg incident.

Phebe Merritt, Lewis Brower's daughter, testified that she ran home when she heard about her mother. Her father said that two men, thought to be thieves, entered the room. They swung at him but missed and hit his wife. Lewis chased them naked into the street and then hid in a woodshed for half an hour. He then went to find his grandson, George Merritt. After arriving home, neighbor George Powers was there. Lewis said that thieves chased him into the kitchen—the location of Sarah Ann's bed—and tried to hit him as well. He claimed to have followed footprints two miles to a Black family and reentered the house through a garret window. Deputy Sheriff Solomon Allen debunked Lewis's story, reporting that the window was covered with cobwebs and clearly not opened for a long time.

The crime was sensational by local standards, and the trial was filled with East Meadow spectators. Even before the verdict, the general sentiment was that Brower was guilty as charged. Inquiries from jail about the condition of his livestock—but not his injured wife—did not help Brower's case.

While on trial for attempting to kill his wife, Brower was sued by John Southard, the local undertaker, for failure to pay $37.50 toward his mother-in-law's funeral expenses. Mrs. Baldwin sued her husband for divorce, of course. In one disturbing incident, Brower took his lover to the Queens County Fair and made sure to ride by his wife, laughing at her expense.

Lewis was convicted and served four years at Sing Sing Prison. Following her miraculous physical recovery, Sarah lost much of her memory and went to live in Westbury with her daughter and son-in-law, Elizabeth and Isaac Wilson. After his release from prison, Lewis Brower lived a reclusive life back in East Meadow before dying in 1901.

It gets even more complicated and more disturbing. Lewis Brower's son, Parmenus, married Mary Alice Bedell around 1872 but, sticking to the family tradition, fell in love with another woman named Kate Smith, née Baldwin—Mary Jane's sister. Yes, you read that correctly. The younger Brower fell in love with the sister of his father's lover. The key problem is that Kate was married to Valentine Smith, who caught his wife eloping in a wagon with Parmenus. Smith chased the pair, but Brower shot him and was convicted of second-degree assault in September 1887. Lewis served prison time with his son in Sing Sing.

But there's more. Parmenus and Mary were living in the Ridgewood (Wantagh) area with Mary's mother, Maria Bedell, who made headlines for a high-profile late-in-life marriage-for-money arrangement with Solomon Southard that quickly went south when neither partner held up his or her bargain to die quickly and leave their estate to the other. Parmenus and

Mary's fourteen-year-old son, Harry, was an inmate in a juvenile reformatory, the New York House of Refuge.

In an unscrupulous move, lawyer George Mott ensured payment for legal services by obtaining power of attorney from Lewis while he was incarcerated. While Sarah Ann was still living there, Mott sold off their livestock and property and ended up owning the farm by February, although he gave Sarah Ann ten acres and a home. He continued to counsel Brower in prison who, upon release, persuaded Mott to pay more for the property.

Perhaps the old residents of Hogshead—descendants of the earliest town settlers—did indeed live up to the community's reputation.

Sarah Ann Barnum, Woman on a Mission

The wealthiest resident of East Meadow in the nineteenth century was Peter Crosby Barnum (1816–1889), who owned a clothing store called P.C. Barnum and Company between 194 and 200 Chatham Square in Manhattan. The important retail center operated from 1845 until 1891. He also owned a farm west of Barnum (Merrick) Avenue. When P.C. married in 1846, he became the largest landowner in Queens County. The 1860 "Productions of Agriculture" schedule shows Barnum farming on 2,100 acres and eclipsing all other East Meadow farmers by huge margins in acreage, land value, livestock ownership and produce output. Barnum was a major grower of rye, corn, oats, potatoes and buckwheat. Twenty sheep produced eighty pounds of wool in 1860 alone, before his operations and family landholdings expanded even further. A gristmill and icehouse at the Meadow Brook served the entire community.

Peter's wife, Sarah Ann, was a commanding figure who managed the farm when P.C. was in Manhattan. Born in 1814, she was the daughters of farmers/innkeepers Thomas and Susan Baldwin (from, appropriately, the hamlet named after them). She raised purebred horses and cattle, ran a dairy and grew vegetables. From her fourth-floor cupola, Mrs. Barnum looked out on her estate and oversaw scores of employees. Census records from 1870 show at least thirty workers and their families living on the farm itself. Sarah Ann also raised two children, Joshua Willets and Kate Vail, in the antebellum period. The children lived at the family's tony Upper East Side Manhattan residence and attended fine private schools. Kate Vail went to Miss Haines' School for Girls in Grammercy Park before taking up residence with her parents in East Meadow. Sarah Ann had two older

Peter Crosby Barnum, circa 1865.
Nassau County Archives.

children from an earlier marriage to Samuel R. Carman: Sarah Frances and Anglesea. She was predeceased by their son, Samuel. Peter had an older daughter, Orra Clarissa, born to late first wife Frances Maria Barnum, a cousin from Putnam County.

Sarah Ann Barnum was an economic force in East Meadow but was also impressive and influential throughout the town of Hempstead. Mrs. Barnum was a civic leader, a visionary and a politician—all in the years before women had the right to vote. She was a founding member of the Queens County Agricultural Society and yielded political power through that position, although her husband was its president. She regularly attended Town of Hempstead meetings and became known as the "eighth member" of the board of supervisors. Apparently, no candidate for public office endorsed by Barnum lost his election, and her brother Francis became the county treasurer. Most notably, Sarah Ann Barnum convinced the townsfolk and members of her agricultural society to sell the common lands of the Hempstead Plains to Alexander Stewart. Its subdivision would fund public education and welfare initiatives while paving the way for the creation of Garden City and other developments. Barnum worked with Supervisor Carman Cornelius to orchestrate the sale. His daughter Mary became Sarah Ann's trusted servant.

The political "boss" had the wherewithal to assist others. Sarah Ann became best known for her philanthropic efforts, especially when she purchased Hog Island (between Oceanside and Long Beach) in 1874 for the purpose of creating the Queens County Poor Farm. The farm would give destitute residents a place to grow food and be productive in society in exchange for food and lodging. Knowing that the island was for sale, she boarded a rowboat at night, put up more than $13,000 of her own money and purchased the land before other interested parties had a chance. She then turned over the property to the county at no profit. The island, which enabled poor residents to leave the squalid conditions of the older almshouses, was subsequently renamed Barnum Island in her honor. She created the Ladies' Summer Festival as a yearly fundraiser for the Poor Farm and served on the Committee on Adult Able-Bodied Paupers and the Local Visiting Committee, responsible for oversight of local charities. Barnum's work with the farm became controversial when she was accused of using its inmates for personal gain.

The superintendents of jails and workhouses in Kings and Queens Counties seemed to answer to nobody in particular; their jobs and the conditions of the facilities were at the whim of political machines. This was, after all, the Gilded Age—the era of Boss Tweed and Tammany Hall in nearby New York City. Keepers at jails and poorhouses were paid based on the number of inmates; corrupt politicians made fortunes transferring the unfortunate to facilities run by their friends. In 1876, Barnum, through her committee work, helped uncover abuses at Barnum Island and in other county institutions, including improper financial management and sexual impropriety by male residents and the house's keeper, Charles Wright. Conditions improved, but an 1891 exposé in the *Brooklyn Daily Eagle* described the situation in Queens County poorhouses as "scandalous and wasteful of public money."

Although Barnum was a champion for the poor, she was accused of using her political influence—and Barnum Island—for personal profit. She created "palatial quarters" there but was known to use laborers on her 2,500-acre East Meadow farm each summer. One such farmer plucked from Barnum Island was Henry Brecht, described as a "quarrelsome…tramp." On November 12, 1882, Brecht and several other laborers visited William Roth's Saloon in Hempstead Village. One of the men, Joseph Maas, Barnum's blacksmith, asked Brecht to vacate the saloon's rear room so he could drink with some women. Maas was known to abuse alcohol but had no history of violence. The two left separately. Nobody recalled an argument of any kind, yet when Brecht returned to the farm, he seemed to plan revenge for the annoyance in the saloon. Brecht went to Maas's room over the blacksmith shop but found he was not yet home; he then went angrily to the carpenter's room, where Charlie Bentz kicked him out. Maas later found Brecht waiting outside his gate. Brecht began to stab Maas, succeeding in plunging the knife in his face and tearing his clothes. Maas fired two shots from the revolver he had been carrying, and one entered Brecht's head. Brecht pulled Maas to the ground, but Maas got up, asked a coworker to help dress his wounds and went to bed. The next morning, Brecht's body was found in a pool of blood. Joshua Barnum determined that he was not dead and called on the local physician. He and the coroner determined that Brecht was paralyzed and would not live. Several days later, Brecht died, and Maas was turned over to law enforcement. A jury of Barnum's neighbors was empaneled, and they put laborers on the witness stand that December and concluded that the homicide was justified. This was not the first alcohol-induced homicide on the farm: in 1876, laborer Frank Evans pillaged Nathaniel Holmes's house near the mill before punching and chasing him, presumably in a drunken stupor. Holmes shot Evans dead.

In 1888, ten-year-old orphaned boy Andrew Smith came to live with Joseph Smith of East Meadow. In this arrangement, he was cared for and schooled locally rather than live at Barnum Island. The county paid Smith six dollars per month for providing room and board. Sarah Ann Barnum, familiar with the arrangement, thought the boy useful for her own plantation. When he was eleven years old, Barnum and her attorney created an agreement with county officials that indentured Andrew to her as a worker until his twenty-first birthday. At that time, young Smith was to be given fifty dollars in cash, two suits and freedom. Meanwhile, he would be part of the Barnum family. According to newspaper accounts from 1889, the boy was given chores usually done by a grown man. He did not enjoy meals with the family and was not sent to school or church, as promised. Andrew ran away to Joseph Smith's house; the poorhouse's superintendent, Mr. Ryder, found him there, and a physical struggle ensued. The boy was briefly returned to Barnum, but he ran away again in February 1889, this time to his grandfather Ira Smith, in nearby Greenwich Point (now Roosevelt). Andrew and his grandfather constantly attempted to evade Mr. Cornwell, overseer of the Barnum farm, and the matter made its way into the court system. Mrs. Barnum realized that she could not forcibly keep the boy and asked the judge to decide on a writ of habeas corpus, which forced Ira Smith to appear with Andrew. According to newspaper accounts, Judge Garretson set the boy free. The indenture clearly violated the U.S. Constitution. The little boy went to live with his grandfather, and Barnum continued her farming and philanthropic work.

Ironically, in 1899, when the newly formed Nassau County desired to close the poorhouse at Barnum Island, its residents refused to leave. Food and lodging conditions were so good that the "hoboes" hired a lawyer to fight their eviction. Others came in droves to the farm demanding room and board. The county supervisors had to stand guard on the road to Barnum Island and turn people away by force. Mrs. Barnum's positive legacy was so strong that the 1889 case has become merely a footnote in local history.

Later in life, Barnum helped found the Mineola Asylum for the Insane, which took over the old Queens County Courthouse building. When she died in 1893, an obituary in the *Brooklyn Daily Eagle* claimed that Barnum was

Sarah Ann Barnum, circa 1865.
Patrick Barnum.

"one of the best known women in Queens [C]ounty" and "a power in Hempstead town affairs." She established an interest-bearing account for her servant, Mary Cornelius. Had she been alive a generation later, Sarah Ann Barnum would have likely befriended East Meadow's "best-known" early twentieth-century feminist and suffragette, Alva Belmont.

Following Sarah Barnum's death, Joshua Willets Barnum, Kate Vail Barnum and Sarah Frances (Carman) Willets inherited the farm properties that straddled Merrick Avenue (also known as Barnum Avenue or Whaleneck Road). By far the largest was the main Barnum estate on the west side, running from the Belmont and Brisbane estates at Front Street south to North Jerusalem Road. This huge farm tract became Joshua's property, while other parcels on the east side of Merrick Avenue (and farther east toward Jerusalem and farther south toward Merrick) became property of his sisters. Kate eventually moved to the Hotel Bossert on Montague Street in Brooklyn Heights, passing away in Manhattan in 1942.

It was at Meadow Brook Farm, the Barnum estate, that Joshua, an alumnus of the New York City Free Academy (the college preparatory high school that became the City College of New York), continued his parents' work as a farmer and major employer. His farm manager, Danish-born Christian Peterson, oversaw a staff that included laborers, servants, a cook and a maid. Many of these workers continued to live on the property. Joshua became a well-known judge of horses, particularly among the Long Island hunting and riding set. He married Mary Richmond Taylor in 1879. Their daughter Maie helped save the mansion in 1904 when she saw flames shooting out of the third floor. Maie alarmed the farmhands and organized them into a bucket brigade, while a friend, Edna Losea, ran a fire house, attached it to a hydrant and doused the fire. Newspapers marveled at the "girl firefighters," but Maie, who débuted to New York society in 1902, was an expert whip. When she married Frederick Leighton Harris in 1905, the wedding was covered in the society pages of New York newspapers—it took place in the drawing room of the Barnum mansion

Barnum Mansion, just west of Merrick Avenue between today's Eric Lane and Andrews Lane. *Nassau County Archives.*

and was followed by a reception of four hundred guests. Mr. Harris died there the following summer.

In 1906, Joshua Barnum died, and George Munson took over farm operations, which also featured Meadow Brook Club polo matches. His father, John, intended to raise horses and hounds for hunting. John Munson, who died suddenly just after leasing the property in 1908, was a prominent member of Confederate colonel John Mosby's "Partisan Rangers" guerrilla fighters in his native Virginia. On September 10, 1910, a terrible fire broke out in Munson's largest horse barn. As George tried unsuccessfully to free all the horses, he almost became trapped in the smoke. His favorite horse, Accountant, intelligently worked his way out of a small door, and Munson was able to escape. He came out of an unconscious state and credited the horse with saving his life. Fourteen horses were saved, including those of famous neighbor Willie K. Vanderbilt Jr. Other owners, including many club members, were not as lucky.

Meadow Brook Park and the Oasis

The Oasis, near The Plain Road and Stewart Avenue in Salisbury, was the longtime home of Emily Louise Ladenburg (née Stevens), widow of Moritz Adolph (Adolf) Ladenburg. Adolf was born in Frankfurt am Main and was descended from a wealthy German Jewish banking family. Ladenburg joined with Ernst Thalmann, an American banker, to form Ladenburg Thalmann after coming to America in 1876. In time, the company grew into a major international financial services firm. Emily came from a distinguished family, and her father was a bank president in Lawrence. The Ladenburgs—fans of horseback riding, fox hunting and polo—married in 1884. The Oasis featured a tall windmill and was named for its abundance of trees, a rarity on the nineteenth-century Hempstead Plains.

On April 14, 1888, Adolf Ladenburg incorporated the Meadow Brook Park Improvement Company with the object of "the subdivision of lands in Hempstead, and improving and selling them." He partnered with several other prominent men, including Elliott Roosevelt and August Belmont. The Meadow Brook Park Colony, as it came to be called, was popular with friends from the nearby Meadow Brook Hunt Club on Merrick Avenue. About a dozen houses planned in the spring of 1890 were built next to trees imported from Europe. Residents stylishly rode horses on The Oasis's Ladenburg (or Meadow Brook) Race Track.

Adolf, overworked and sickly, was instructed by his doctor to visit the warmer climate of Florida. In 1896, Adolf was lost at sea, supposedly swept overboard a Ward Line steamer during a rough storm as he was traveling from Nassau in the Bahamas. Emily inherited a $7.5 million fortune and continued to live at The Oasis. In the years after her husband's death, Emily, descendant of a Tammany Hall founder, became a real New York socialite. She was frequently engaged, although none of her many engagements resulted in a second marriage. The whole "Meadowbrook Set" was abuzz in 1899 when a rumor emerged that Emily might take up with her neighbor across Valentines Road, expert horseman Ralph Nicholson Ellis, Meadow Brook Club's master of the fox hounds and college friend of Theodore Roosevelt. Ellis was widowed from his wife, Elizabeth Warder, with whom he lived at a mansion called Bunga Fields in Brookville. At the turn-of-the-century, Ladenburg leased The Oasis to Camilla Beach, widow of Charles Havemeyer, Sugar Trust socialite. Frederick Beach, a broker, was active in the polo set.

As with many society ladies of her day, Mrs. Ladenburg took up charitable and progressive causes, especially those that concerned women and children. In November 1917, she penned a piece in the *New York Times*, encouraging school lunch for all children in the city. "It is necessary," she wrote, "for the children attending public schools to have one good hot meal a day, and there should be a lunch service owned and managed by every public school."

Emily Ladenburg in the British tank *Britannia*, which visited New York City in the winter of 1918, following World War I. *Bain Collection, Library of Congress.*

She encouraged people of means to donate to private charities such as the Association for Improving the Condition of the Poor, which would work with schools to provide lunches. No records exist that show Ladenburg took up the matter in her local East Meadow Public School.

Emily Ladenburg is most known for "liberating" women in the equestrian world due to her reluctance to ride sidesaddle. Sidesaddle was the traditional, proper way for a genteel lady to ride a horse: she would need to be helped onto the horse by a gentleman, and she was essentially helpless once on the animal, having no means of control. Progressive women saw sidesaddle riding as another sign of masculine oppression. A popular story involving Ladenburg centers on Sarasota Springs, New York, in the summer of 1902. There, at an equestrian event, Emily appeared in scandalous clothing—a split skirt—that would allow her to comfortably and expertly ride horses astride, as men did. Although she was not the first woman to do so, her position in society (particularly in fashionable New York City, Long Island and Newport, Rhode Island) helped the phenomenon spread. Her whereabouts and parties were covered heavily in newspapers of record, and she was described in the 1907 Society journal *The Scrap Book* as "one of the beautiful women of New York." The Long Island Motor Parkway was constructed abutting the Ladenburg property in 1908. Friends and family members would come watch the Vanderbilt Cup Races.

Misfortune befell Ladenburg several times. Her daughter Eugenie "May" was nearly kidnapped in 1906. Emily was injured in a fall in 1914. In 1925, she was hit by a car in front of the Madison Hotel on East Fifty-Eighth Street in Manhattan.

One home on the Ladenburg property, still standing at 730 Boelsen Drive, became known as "The Box." It was occupied by John "Jack" de Saulles, who was gunned down on his porch by ex-wife Blanca Errázuriz on August 3, 1917. John, socialite and former Yale football star, married Blanca—known for her beauty—in 1911 and had one son: John Jr. The marriage broke apart after taxi dancer and future movie star Rodolfo Guglielmi testified to John's infidelity. The enraged John had Guglielmi arrested for immoral behavior; controversy surrounding the case led to the actor adopting stage name Rudolph Valentino. John's refusal to accept a joint-custody agreement led to the shooting, after which Blanca exclaimed, "I killed him and I'm glad I did it. He refused to give me my child, although he was ordered by the court." She planned on taking the boy, who witnessed the murder, to Chile that November.

Left: John de Saulles, 1901. *Library of Congress.*

Right: Blanca de Saulles, circa 1910–15. *Library of Congress.*

A sensational trial typical of the period ensued at Mineola. Attorney Henry Uterhart planned an "emotional insanity" defense and argued that an old skull fracture led to her altered mental state, exacerbated by the pain of losing custody of her child. The defense leaned heavily on anti-chauvinistic sentiments and portrayed Blanca as a victim of a loveless marriage who endured years of humiliation and neglect. On December 1, after only one and a half hours of deliberation, Blanca was acquitted. Jurors made it clear that they were fighting for her. John Jr. was returned to her custody, and the two moved west.

Following Ladenburg's death in 1937, The Box and surrounding lands were sold to Frederick William Boelsen. The Oasis and The Box were sold and divided for postwar development in 1950 and 1954. May Ladenburg, in a break with her late mother's progressivism, later supported controversial political causes such as the pro-eugenics Pioneer Fund. She married attorney Preston Davie, who collected historical documents about the South.

Theodore Roosevelt's brother, Elliott, built his ten-acre Meadow Brook Park country home, Half Way Nirvana, north of Valentines Road. Elliott, a loving father but chronic alcoholic, traveled with Adolf Ladenburg and enjoyed the fast club life, which led to accidents and pain medication

Above: The Box at The Oasis. *Nassau County Archives.*

Opposite: Half Way Nirvana, 1889. *National Archives.*

dependency. His mental state deteriorated, resulting in his brother opening a lunacy inquiry in 1891. While he was confined to a French asylum, his wife, Anna, sued for divorce. He returned on the promise of further treatment and distance from public affairs (so as not to cause a scandal within the political family), but when his wife and son died a year later, Elliott could not recover from his addiction. He died in 1894. Daughter (Anna) Eleanor (1884–1962), who spent her childhood at the estate between 1888 and 1892, grew up to become first lady and an international rights activist.

Polo star of the 1920s and 1930s Gerald Dempsey owned the former Ellis estate, valued at $150,000, before he was thirty-five. Russian royalty turned stable operator Prince Gregory Gagarin and his sister, Princess Sophie, settled on Old Country Road at Westbury Road. Gagarin and his family came by way of France and were active in the Holy Trinity Orthodox Church in the Slavic community near Front Street.

A YELLOW JOURNALIST IN EAST MEADOW

Remember the Spanish-American War of 1898? No? Surely you "Remember the *Maine!*" The battle cry you might remember from junior high was the work of "yellow journalists" of the 1890s. Without them, including East Meadow's Arthur Brisbane (1864–1936), we may never have acquired Puerto Rico, Guam and the Philippines (returned on July 4, 1946). By the late nineteenth century, two New York City newspapers, Joseph Pulitzer's *New York World* and William Randolph Hearst's *New York Journal*, were competing for readers by printing increasingly sensational headlines, stories and pictures. Although reporting was faulty by standards of the time, or even purposely inaccurate, this competition often shaped public opinion about national or international events. Brisbane worked for both publications but rose to become the managing editor of Hearst's *Journal*. Pulitzer and Hearst made enormous sums of money, which was not shared commensurately with their staff or "Newsies" sales boys. Ironically, Brisbane's father, Albert, was a social reformer. Yellow journalism got its start exposing the evils of urban society just prior to the Progressive era, but it profited greatly from exploiting the working class, foreigners and, indirectly, military personnel. Later investigations suggested that the *Maine*'s boiler exploded and that Spain probably had nothing to do with the tragedy, but those facts don't sell newspapers.

Brisbane wrote a regular column, "Today," which was reportedly seen by up to 30 million readers due to its widespread syndication in hundreds of newspapers. Luckily for Brisbane, his pay was tied to newspaper sales, and he achieved significant financial success. Just for good measure, he also made a fortune in New York City real estate and donated his Pierce Arrow touring car to the East Meadow Fire Department. Brisbane was known to be a great horseman and farmer and loved his second home, Long Island. At the time, his neighbors in East Meadow were also horsemen and farmers. The influential financier J.P. Morgan owned a large tract of land called Hempstead Farm for these purposes just down the street. Brisbane would commute by train to work in New York City; Salisbury Plains Station was walking distance from his home in current-day Eisenhower Park. Arthur Brisbane's properties were located at the southwest and northeast corners of Merrick Avenue and Front Street (where his father-in-law, Seward Cary, lived east of Brookholt), at the southeast corner of Merrick Avenue and Hempstead Turnpike and at the northwest corner of Hempstead Turnpike and Newbridge Avenue. He also owned a tract of land on the east side of Newbridge Road that he donated to the school district. In 1915, Hearst lawyer/ Brisbane associate State Supreme Court Justice Clarence Shearn and his family were living alongside Brisbane.

Arthur Brisbane. *Library of Congress.*

Brisbane's personal attorney was Yale- and Columbia-educated Geoffrey Konta

(1887–1942). Konta was also the attorney for William Randolph Hearst, one of the major newspaper owners for whom Brisbane worked. Geoffrey and Phyllis Konta lived at the northwest corner of Newbridge Avenue and Hempstead Turnpike, on property that abutted one of Brisbane's several holdings. When you're a controversial journalist, it's best to keep your lawyer close at hand, right? The estate he built on the property was called East Meadows. As with most other Gilded Age personalities, the Kontas owned another fashionable residence at 290 Park Avenue in Manhattan. They split their time between New York City and Long Island, appearing in the "Dilatory Domiciles" summer social registers by the Social Register Association. These were essentially listings of prominent (read: rich) ladies and gentlemen with whom you might dine or sail. Konta spent his final days in East Meadow. The estate was purchased by Nassau County and absorbed into what is now Eisenhower Park. Brisbane's grandson, also named Arthur, was the fourth public editor of the *New York Times*.

ALONG HEMPSTEAD-BETHPAGE TURNPIKE IN 1900

The Rowehls, German-born truck farmers, lived at the current East Meadow–Levittown border. Just west farmed Albert Berg, whose younger brother Peter Jr. lived on Front Street. Their father, Peter Sr., was born in Denmark. In the nineteenth century, the elder Peter ran a saloon at the corner of Front Street and Merrick Avenue. West of the Berg family farm resided tobacconist Frances Calcagnino and his family, who came to East Meadow following his wife's untimely death. He suffered a devastating barn fire in 1897. J.P. Morgan–backed Hempstead Farm was just west of Newbridge Road, initially the country estate of Thomas Terry.

Richard Lowden, fifty-eight, was listed in the U.S. Census as the head of household for his farm just west of Morgan's property at Carman Avenue. Richard lived with his wife, Mary, and his children: Florence, Addie, Jessie, Walter, Bertha and William. Lowden was quite active in local Republican politics (placed in charge of town roads) and was commissioner of East Meadow Hall in its earliest days. He was also trustee of the East Meadow School in the 1880s. Lowden married into one of Long Island's oldest families, the Carmans. Two boarders lived with the Lowdens and worked as farm laborers: John Brand and Charles Simmon. Simmon was born in Switzerland, moved to the United States in 1890 and became a naturalized citizen.

Above: Carman-Lowden Homestead in 1887 (painting by R. Bond). The Carmans, residing in the town of Hempstead since its seventeenth-century inception, managed the only inn on the Hempstead-Bethpage Turnpike, which ran to Farmingdale.

Opposite page: Western section of East Meadow showing landowners in 1896. "Whaleneck Avenue" is Merrick Avenue.

Just west of the Lowdens lived Owen and Elizabeth Reilly (or Riley)—ages sixty-nine and seventy, respectively—and their three single adult children named James, Rose and Julia. The Reillys moved to the United States from Ireland in 1850 and became farmers in East Meadow.

At the northwest corner of Hempstead Turnpike and Newbridge Avenue, near current-day Park Boulevard, was the estate of George Coggeshall and Elizabeth (Peers) Tatem, ages fifty-five and fifty-four, and three sons. George's aunt Margaret Cleland previously lived on the property and, childless, seems to have co-owned the land with or bequeathed the estate to her sister Sarah's family. Sarah and her second husband, James Richmond, were farming there by 1870. Margaret was said to have lived in East Meadow's largest house aside from that of O.H.P. Belmont, and it was quite the family compound. She was in the first cohort of New York City teachers to receive a pension for her work, having retired as principal of the Bleecker Street School. Margaret's younger sister Rebecca resided with her for the last few years of her life. Sarah's children from her first marriage to Captain Jackson Tatem (from whom she was widowed), including George and his family, lived together.

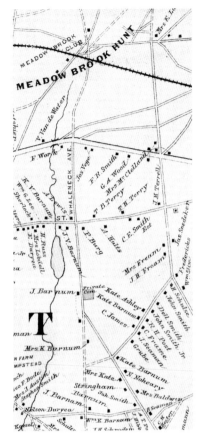

George claimed to be a professional musician—he was a skilled organist in New York City—but was a most interesting and well-known personality in East Meadow. The following year, he would start a stretch as justice of the peace for the Town of Hempstead. He also served as coroner, Masonic leader and, of course, farmer. The Tatems were parents to eleven children, many of whom had already married. One twenty-two-year-old son, Edgar, still lived at home and was listed as a painter. On a corner of the Reilly property, just across from his parents, lived another son, Francis. Frank, as he was known, was twenty-six years old and a painter. He lived with his wife, Ida, twenty-four, and their infant daughter named Agnes. Their home was completed in July 1909.

West of George Tatem's property, south of the turnpike, was the small Wood family farm. George, forty-nine, and Carrie, forty-two, lived there with their seven young children. Next door was the home of Elbert and Sarah Smith, ages fifty-one and fifty, and their seven children. Elbert was a carpenter, and his twenty-seven-year-old single daughter Carrie was a dressmaker.

A PROSPECT AVENUE PROFESSOR

In the nineteenth century, Prospect Avenue was known as Hay Carter's (or Haycarter's) Lane and was sleepier than Hempstead Turnpike, gaining it the nickname "Sleepy Lane." As its name suggests, local farmers would take the country lane to the hay fields. The fields were not far from anybody's homestead because the lane ended at Newbridge Avenue (now East Meadow Avenue). On 1863 Civil War draft records, Samuel Post is listed as a "Hay Carter." He lived on the southeast side of the lane,

Frederick Grubé.

making it possible that it was named for him or his family. Just southwest of Post was the family of Daniel Valentine, a carpenter. The next resident southwest was John Seaman, who also worked as a "Hay Carter." One of the most distinguished residents of Prospect Avenue was Dr. Frederick Grubé.

Frederick Grubé, PhD, LLD, was born in Germany in 1840 and earned two doctorates in Europe (at Bonn University and Trinity College) before settling in the United States in 1870. He married Ellen Gordon the same year and was then a professor in Vermont and at the University of Nebraska. Dr. Grubé was a public school teacher in New York City for more than twenty years, a professor of languages at Boys' High School in Brooklyn. He was also renowned for his works *Dialogues in Latin*, *Latin Ode on Greater New York* and various works in German, French, Spanish and English. Ellen, a decorated musician with a college degree, was an academic and educator in her own right. Frederick Grubé was appointed by New York City mayor Robert Van Wyck as a member of the Commission of Statistics. The Grubés' daughter Eulalia lived in East Meadow. She died at age forty-three in 1919, leaving an estate of $4,128.41 to her half sister, Lillian Johnson, who also lived in the community. Alfred Walsh married a third sister, Maude, and together they built a summer home adjoining their parents.

A laudatory exposé in the *Tammany Times* called Grubé an "unsurpassed" orator and dedicated member of his political party. Indeed, Grubé was an outspoken Democratic political activist who wrote passionately about the need to reform state government, which he thought to be bloated with corrupt legislative committees. "Who cannot see the danger to any man's freedom from an Albany Legislative Committee," he wrote in 1899, "in theory responsible to a majority, which is, in turn, obtusely and wickedly responsible only to itself and oblivion." Grubé believed that parliamentary committees threatened the intent of the Declaration of Independence and separation of powers as outlined in the Constitution. "If free government is to live," he concluded, "Legislative Committees must go!" He wrote fervently about honest and true Tammany men. The Tammany Society, of course, was notorious for its political corruption in the late nineteenth century under Boss Tweed.

After Ellen's death in 1891, Grubé married Marie Emilie Daniel, an aristocratic Louisianan. The Grubés' home on Prospect Avenue, which started out as a country estate during Frederick's working years, was southwest of current-day Coakley Street. The main house, Gothic Cottage, appears to be the location of today's East Meadow Jewish Center. The Grubés were mid-level society figures. The professor assisted with charity events, such as the 1892 "Six Old Maids Bazaar" to benefit the East Meadow Sunday School of the Methodist Episcopal Church. His wife helped raise funds for the Sunday School Library.

In 1907–8, the New York City Department of Education hosted a series of public lectures. Dr. Grubé gave two lectures in German and English on Goethe's *Faust* and Frederick the Great. He also gave an English-language lecture on the history of Holland. Frederick died in 1918 after a weeklong bout with pneumonia. Emilie passed away ten years later. Frederick and Emilie had two daughters, one of whom, Lillian, lived in East Meadow.

BROOKHOLT MANSION

While East Meadow is not the first hamlet that comes to mind when one thinks of Long Island Gold Coast–style mansions, Front Street was certainly home to one truly impressive estate in its halcyon days. This mansion was home to Oliver Hazard Perry (O.H.P.) Belmont (1858–1908) and his second wife, Alva Erskine Smith Vanderbilt (1853–1933). The couple lived just north of the Barnum estate in a home they had commissioned and built in 1897, a year after their marriage. The house, designed by architect Richard Howland Hunt, was a Colonial Revival–style mansion. In keeping with the convention of all the society families of the time, the house had a name: Brookholt. The "brook" refers to the (East) Meadow Brook, which meandered through the property very close to the parkway that adopted its name. The suffix "holt" means "wood." Brookholt was a Gilded Age masterpiece.

Originally a southern belle from Mobile, Alabama, Alva became a regular socialite in the Northeast. Vacationing in Newport, Rhode Island, made it possible for Alva to find her first husband, William Kissam Vanderbilt. She eventually owned nine homes and inherited a small fortune after her divorce. Starting near the bottom of the social ladder and forever attempting to climb it, Alva orchestrated a loveless marriage between her daughter Consuelo Vanderbilt and Charles Spencer-Churchill, an English duke. Her new husband, O.H.P., was the son of August Belmont of the Rothschild banking

Brookholt Mansion. *Art Kleiner.*

enterprise. August Belmont, originally a German Jew, made his fortune financing Japanese expansion after his father-in-law, Commodore Matthew Perry, had opened that country to American trade. O.H.P. was a financier and U.S. congressman. August Belmont Jr., his brother, was a financier and bank trustee who lived close by at Hempstead's Blemton Manor. He was also friends with William Kissam Vanderbilt, Alva's first husband.

Together, the Belmonts created one of the "show places of America." Brookholt had 240 acres of gardens, orchards and trees, along with stables and other buildings. The pair became very progressive. Alva hired workmen to create two artificial lakes in 1900. They went on strike for higher wages and shorter hours, which Alva granted. O.H.P. began a political campaign against robber barons of the day, and Alva became a prominent suffragette. Since New York State allowed women to vote in 1917, three years before the passage of the Nineteenth Amendment granting national suffrage, she sought to inspire women by getting involved with local politics. She also utilized her position of wealth and power to rebuild the Methodist Episcopal church on Newbridge Avenue and argue for higher teacher salaries, particularly for women.

Life at Brookholt was exciting. More than just a home, Brookholt hosted social gatherings and local fundraisers for causes championed by the Belmonts. The estate increased in size to eight hundred acres. Alva's son, Willie K. Vanderbilt II, spent considerable time at the East Meadow home because of its easy access to wide-open spaces—places to race his beloved modern toys: fancy, fast automobiles. Willie K.'s enthusiasm for motor vehicles was well known. He established the Vanderbilt Cup Races in 1904, which attracted large numbers of spectators and tourists. The races took place on public roads like Hempstead Turnpike, which abutted the northern end of the Brookholt estate. Although races brought lodgers to East Meadow inns and stimulated the local economy, the distaste for danger on public highways eventually led to the construction of the Long Island Motor Parkway for the fast-paced events and touring. It was, according to historian and fellow East Meadow native Howard Kroplick, "the first parkway built exclusively for the automobile and part of the courses for the 1908 to 1910 Vanderbilt Cup Races." Access to the Motor Parkway was limited; when not used for racing, private motorists could pay a two-dollar toll for the privilege of driving on the private road. The entrance, Meadow Brook Lodge, was just west of Merrick Avenue and north of Stewart Avenue. It was designed by John Russell Pope and constructed in time for the 1908 race. Pope had designed an elaborate farmhouse at Brookholt two years earlier that would become important to Alva after her husband's death.

Across Front Street from the main house sat the Brookholt Winter Gardens. The buildings at the gardens were truly impressive; they were equally as ornate as the house itself. The gardens sported a huge greenhouse-type structure

Alva Belmont, circa 1910. *Bain Collection, Library of Congress.*

At work on Belmont's girl farm, with the winter gardens in background, 1911. Alva Belmont designed the outfits herself, which included hats and long blue skirts, as a mix of femininity and utility. *Bain Collection, Library of Congress.*

and windmill. After O.H.P. Belmont's 1908 death from complications from appendicitis, the widowed Alva decided to use her gardens and land for the advancement of women's equality. Known as the Brookholt Agricultural School for Women, or simply Mrs. Belmont's Farm for Women, the charitable venture sought to attract young ladies who had heretofore labored in New York City factories and bring them to the countryside. Out here, she thought, these ladies, known as "farmerettes," might learn how to farm the land and become self-sufficient. They would then be able to move to cleaner, safer areas and use their economic independence to liberate themselves in society. Alva paid them a few dollars a week and provided room, board and practical—not theoretical—lessons under director Laura Dutton Williams. She thought it would help lead to equal pay for equal work. The farm school was a highly publicized endeavor but lasted only one year (1911).

Alva became an outspoken suffragette and used Brookholt as the base of local parades, marches and rallies, while also using her Newport Marble House mansion for public lectures on women's suffrage. She created the Political Equality Association, a very inclusive group of militantly pro-suffrage supporters, and used her East Meadow home as its part-time headquarters. Belmont was often at odds with larger, more established organizations working toward the same goals, but she became very close with feminist Alice Paul. She created an excellent working relationship with African American leaders in Harlem, a rarity for the day. Alva empowered women to vote in local elections, as women of New York State were already enfranchised when the vote involved local representation and taxation issues. She was elected to the position of East Meadow School District trustee on May 3, 1911. Mrs. Belmont ran unopposed, which she did not expect, since she was only the second woman to be a school trustee on Long Island.

In 1915, Brookholt was sold to Alexander Smith Cochran, who in turn sold to Coldstream Golf Club. During Prohibition, the house became a front for the illegal manufacture of alcoholic beverages. When Nassau County police raided the operation in June 1933, they found a ten-thousand-gallon still in the ballroom, set up in an opulent fashion. The mansion burned down on March 2, 1934, a year after Alva Belmont's death. Today, Mitchel Manor occupies the same lot.

PHOENIX LODGE AND JACQUES THE FIRST, EMPEROR OF ALL THE SAHARAS

Henri Jacques Lebaudy of Salisbury, how important you must have been!

What does one do when he has too much money and too much time on his hands? How about start a new country, crown himself emperor and plan a coronation with fake flowers? Surely your loyal subjects bowed down at your feet as you enjoyed sitting on the massive porch of Phoenix Lodge, your royal estate. The citizens of your made-up country, the Empire of the Sahara, must have gleefully collected the stamps and coins featuring palm trees, bees, crowns and your regal name, Jacques I du Sahara. Did your "imperial ensign" fly high when you "abdicated" the throne to move to New York?

Jacques Lebaudy was born into a wealthy family, titans of the French sugar industry. After 1873, he made even more money as the head of a company controlling mines in Huanchaca, Bolivia. In 1903, Lebaudy took his armored yacht, *Frasquita*; two other vessels; and a crew of men to explore and claim the Sahara on the west coast of Morocco. He named an area where they landed the Bay of Free Exchange and intended to plant a capital named Troja near Cape Juby. Lebaudy sent five sailors to claim the land in his name, but the sailors were captured and ransomed. When Lebaudy would not pay, France sent a rescue party to retrieve the men.

Lebaudy was wanted by the French government for his escapades that resulted in kidnapping and international confusion, but he fled to London. It was in London where Lebaudy purchased a throne, donned royal garb, lived in a hotel and hired a huge entourage of men and women to follow him around, take pictures and run the affairs of his fake state. When plans fell through, the emperor moved to his second-best land, the northern section of East Meadow, Long Island. Ironically, the region Lebaudy attempted to claim remains disputed territory to this day. Had he been more successful, perhaps a fully recognized government would exist in western Sahara. He did not attempt to colonize Salisbury but did keep uniformed messenger boys as guards.

Lebaudy was married in France in 1896 but was the cause of much suffering for Augustine Léonie Marguerite (Margaret) Dellière, his wife, and their daughter, Jacqueline. On multiple occasions, Mrs. Lebaudy reported that her husband physically assaulted them. He was sent to an insane asylum, for the first time, after a fit of rage involving his wife and the sale of some livestock.

The Lebaudys lived in a fifty-room mansion on Valentines Road named Phoenix Lodge, which they bought in 1913 for $39,000. The house itself was built in 1898 by three members the Eustis family (siblings James, George and Marie), who were Confederate supporters and politicians. The original home burned in December 1897; only a piano was saved from the conflagration. Eventually, James Biddle Eustis became ambassador extraordinary and plenipotentiary to France in the 1890s and moved to New York. Aside from running the farm, the French-born George was a theatrical manager. Eleven servants lived on the property with Eustis in 1900: a nurse, butler, valet, cook, laundress, coachman, stableman and several maids. It was quite the multicultural farm, with workers from England, France, Japan, Ireland, Sweden and Finland! A new barn was constructed in 1902 following a fire.

In August 1915, Jacques was angered when Mrs. Edward Smith drove by his estate on Westbury Road. He irrationally blocked the road with tree trunks, wagons and hay, causing Smith to contact the sheriffs. When they arrived, Lebaudy proclaimed, "I am the Emperor of the Saharas. Surrender!" He commanded his messenger boys, decked out in imperial uniforms, to charge at the officers. After a wild chase on horseback, Lebaudy said to Sheriff Stephen Pettit, "I surrender to the United States Government. I am Jacques Lebaudy, Emperor of Sahara, and I give up to you." He ended up in the Knickerbocker Sanitarium in Amityville, from which he fled days later.

The following month, Marguerite called the sheriff because her husband telephoned from a hotel in New York City to say that they were not married. He threatened to send four men to "clean the place out" and attempted to cut off the utilities and change the locks on the doors to force her out. Jacques took out advertisements claiming that "a French woman of no social standing has been for some time attempting to pose as being wedded to him." He was apparently worried about her debt. In the style of the day,

East Meadow in 1923, featuring O.L. Schwencke developments, Salisbury estates, Lannin's holdings, the Motor Parkway and the Central Line. E. Belcher Hyde real estate map. *Art Kleiner/Howard Kroplick/Scott Eckers.*

newspapers printed sensational stories about their nuptials. One month later, the increasingly mad Jacques found himself confined at a mental institution in Kings Park for ten days.

On January 11, 1919, Marguerite shot and killed Jacques at Phoenix Lodge. Accounts of the circumstances differ, but all are disturbing. Secondary-source accounts claim that Jacques was attempting to burn down the house; others claim that he was attempting to seduce his teenage daughter, Jacqueline, so that he may have sons to carry on his "royal" title. In self-defense, his wife shot him five times. Jacques Lebaudy was found with a loaded revolver in his coat. Marguerite happily confessed and told Constable Charles O'Conner that "he deserved it." A jury refused to indict Mrs. Lebaudy. She and her daughter received most of his estate, valued at $13 million.

Phoenix Lodge and sensational headlines regarding "strange happenings" in the aftermath of the Lebaudy case, 1922. *From the* Buffalo Times Sun.

Jacques Lebaudy is buried at St. Brigid's Cemetery in Westbury. In October 1922, Marguerite married Henri Sudreau, and Jacqueline married Henri's son, Roger. They had a double wedding—largely to make sure the money stayed in the family—and moved to France.

Phoenix Lodge was robbed in 1921 and subsequently fell into disrepair before being sold to Lannin Realty Company at a tax auction in July 1926. The owner hired a caretaker named Thomas Pearson to look after the property, but he set up an elaborate still in the house during the Prohibition era and was arrested by federal agents. A fire destroyed farm buildings in 1935. Suburban homes sit on the property today, built by Herbert Sadkin in 1953 as the first three sections of Birchwood at Westbury.

J.J. LANNIN AND THE BUSINESS OF FADS AND HEROES

Drive up Merrick Avenue next to Eisenhower Park and gaze at the beautiful brick structure within the park. Marvel at the park's impressive golf courses. Imagine Lindbergh flying overhead. Could a poor orphan have created such wonders?

A native of Lac-Beauport, Québec, Joseph John Lannin had great aspirations. But these were not easily attainable to the impoverished Canadian boy, so he decided to migrate to the United States to realize his hopes and dreams. Having just lost his father and having no real resources, Lannin left home at age fourteen and began his journey to Boston, Massachusetts—by foot. In 1880, remarkably, he walked 410 miles from his homeland to Boston to pursue the American Dream. That promise held true, and Lannin eventually became a business tycoon worth $7 million. After dabbling in baseball, Lannin purchased the Boston Red Sox. In this capacity, he most notably brought Babe Ruth into the club and developed him as a famous player.

Lannin turned to the real estate industry and developed several hotels. Locally, he built the Garden City Hotel, and a swanky hotel needs a private golf club, which he built at nearby East Meadow. The Salisbury Golf Club was a vast piece of real estate on the Hempstead Plains and comprised five separate courses. The beautiful Salisbury Clubhouse, originally Lannin's Hotel, was located just west of Merrick Avenue. It attracted wealthy, connected socialites and athletes during the Roaring Twenties who could get off the train or parkway just yards away.

Lannin's hotels and golf clubs were located in the heart of Long Island's aviation industry, as airfields straddled his properties. Naturally, he became interested in airplane travel. Being a real estate tycoon, Lannin purchased Roosevelt Field and escorted famous aviator Charles Lindbergh to his plane *Spirit of St. Louis* in 1927. Lindbergh flew right over the Salisbury Golf Club as he lifted off for his historic trip to Paris.

The building in the park, Lannin House, was a wedding gift to J.J.'s daughter, Dorothy Lannin Tunstall. She raised her children, Harry and Joan, at the East Meadow home through the 1930s. The home is angled unusually because it is situated on property that once faced a road that ran northeast toward Oyster Bay.

For unknown reasons, J.J. Lannin fell from the ninth floor of the Hotel Granada, a business he owned in Brooklyn. The full story of his May 1928 demise has never been learned or disclosed.

Salisbury Clubhouse. *Gary Hammond.*

Lannin House. *Nassau County.*

After Lannin's death, his children took over the East Meadow properties. They fell on hard times during the Great Depression, and the golf club was seized for failure to pay back taxes. The property was developed into the county park, which opened in 1944. Salisbury's fourth golf course, initially designed by Devereux Emmet, is now today's Red Course in Eisenhower Park. The clubhouse was used for industrial purposes through the 1980s and later demolished. The Lannin House became the county museum and later housed the Women's Sports Foundation. In 2012, Christopher Tunstall walked and hiked for six weeks in the footsteps of his great-grandfather J.J. to understand what the experience must have been like.

TURN-OF-THE-CENTURY HOTELS

The families operating small hotels in East Meadow in the nineteenth and early twentieth centuries tended to be immigrants from Germany. Unlike most East Meadow residents, who attended the Methodist Episcopal church, these hoteliers were Lutheran or Catholic. Politically, the men tended to associate with the Democratic Party, although most other locals were aligned with the Republican Party. Heinrich (Henry) Schultze, for example, was the proprietor of the East Meadow Hotel and treasurer of the Third District

Democratic Association. Both political parties held meetings at the East Meadow "town hall," the old schoolhouse that had been moved to Schultze's property. Schultze was on the church council of the German Lutheran Epiphany Church of Hempstead.

Henry Alsheimer came from Baden, Germany, in 1882. He and his wife, Pauline, became farmers at Manhasset before the family moved to East Meadow to grow vegetables on Front Street (at today's bowling alley property). Henry's son Edward owned a $23,000 estate there in 1930. From their farm, the Alsheimers transported goods by truck to New York City and Brooklyn markets. Henry ran the nearby Beyerle Hotel from about 1909 until his death. Henry's daughter Katie also lived in East Meadow; his two other sons lived in nearby communities.

East Meadow was usually a safe and orderly place, but its hotels were occasionally the sites of notable offenses. In November 1911, Henry was allegedly assaulted by John Clark, who lived near Smithville South (North Bellmore). Clark, a bartender, allegedly stole six bottles of beer and then hit Alsheimer with one, breaking his nose and causing a head wound. Alsheimer claimed that he was "knocked…senseless" and "[left] for dead on the roadside." After an inquiry, the court set Clark free after

Alsheimer family at Front Street. *Alsheimer family.*

he convinced a local judge that he acted in self-defense. Apparently, Alsheimer pursued Clark, who took off from his hotel with six bottles of beer, and was getting ready to strike him first. Seemingly a jovial fellow, Henry Alsheimer directed his friend Larry Fitzgerald to hire a brass band to play lively music at his funeral. The twenty-piece band did just that when the sixty-six-year-old Alsheimer succumbed to a brief illness in 1917. His estate was valued at $19,000, a reasonable sum of money for the time. Pauline lived until 1931.

The "Noon Inn" at Prospect and Newbridge Avenues was one of the most popular meeting sites in East Meadow. It was built around 1836 by Sylvanus Bedell and subsequently owned by different families, most notably John and Mary Noon, who operated the inn between 1848 and 1861. John Noon became a wealthy real estate investor in the area. The Democratic Club of the town of Hempstead met at the Noon Inn. After operation by the Seaman and Glinsmann families, the property was sold in 1883 to Heinrich and Lena Schultze.

Henry Schultze was known as a "genial proprietor" of the East Meadow Hotel. Great celebrations were thrown at the hotel, such as the 1904 birthday party for his thirteen-year-old daughter, Louisa, that attracted "quite a number of villagers." His hotel was noted in newspapers; when he erected a nice new fence or ran an auction of dry goods, locals observed or attended. In 1902, some neighborhood boys vandalized Schultze's farm wagon, which was left overnight near the Alsheimer property at Front Street. The boys disassembled the wagon and put the wooden boards and wheels up a tree and in the cellar of a former house. A description of this youthful prank and Schultze's angry response ("shaking his fist at persons imaginary and vowing that hereafter he would not leave a wagon on the roadside") took up about three inches of newspaper space, which indicates that there wasn't much news in East Meadow then. Schultze's hotel made the newspapers again in December 1909 when a stranger who took a room for one night skipped out on the bill before breakfast, taking with him thirty-five dollars from another room. After running the East Meadow Hotel for nearly forty years, Schultze sold the property to Andrew and Elizabeth Hoeffner in 1914. He died three years later at age seventy-seven.

Charles Kiestling was born in Germany in 1829, immigrated to the United States in 1851 and built the New Bridge Hotel on Newbridge Road in 1874. He had been living on this property since at least 1859 and earned his living as a shoemaker. The hotel (not to be confused with North Bellmore's Newbridge Hotel or Inn) was just north of the Stewart's Central

Henry Schultze at his bar, circa 1890. *Nassau County Archives.*

Railroad (later LIRR's Central Line), which briefly (1874–76) had a station on the east side of Newbridge Road. After the Newbridge Road Bridge was constructed in the summer of 1908, the Motor Parkway ran between the railroad and the hotel. As a result, the building became a popular place to watch the Vanderbilt Cup Races along the new parkway. Spectators filled the hotel's front lawn and even went up on the roof for a better view. They enjoyed the saloon in the establishment. The New Bridge Hotel was later operated by another German immigrant, Jacob Gaenger, who arrived in the United States in 1882 and married Kiestling's daughter Sophie. Around the turn of the century, the family farmed the land. Jacob Gaenger lived at the hotel with his in-laws, wife and two children, Charley Fred and Louis Jacob. By 1914, fellow German immigrant William Distelkamp had taken over operation of the hotel and continued until October 1917, when the state refused to renew his liquor license. The elder Gaenger became a naturalized citizen in 1923 and subsequently worked in carpentry. Today, the site is on the northwest corner of Newbridge Road and Salisbury Park Drive.

Hoeffner's East Meadow Hotel

Although not a large establishment, the East Meadow Hotel at the intersection of Prospect and Newbridge Avenues became the most well-known hotel in East Meadow and, partly as a result, the center of activity on the southern side of the district. State liquor license documents from 1908 and 1914 list the address as Smithville South and West Roads. The hotel was commonly known as the Noon Inn, since that family owned and operated the property in the mid-nineteenth century, but the property was under the control of its last owners, the Hoeffner family, for the longest amount of time. A small sign located at the property today calls it "Hoeffner's Corner."

Heinrich Schultze sold the property to Andrew and Elizabeth Hoeffner in January 1914. The Hoeffners moved from Fosters Meadow, a German farming community near Elmont, and took over operations of the two-story, six-room East Meadow Hotel, selling Welz & Zerweck Beer at the impressive first-floor bar until Prohibition (1920–33). In 1922, hotel manager Joseph Friar was arrested with keeping a "disorderly" house. He was released on $1,500 bail after pleading not guilty. Since the nation turned "dry" and hotels were dependent on income from the sale of beverages to both travelers and regular customers, the Hoeffners returned full time to farming while raising their seven boys (Edward, Andrew Jr., Ralph, Clifford, Walter, Arthur and Raymond) and two girls (Helen and Matilda) in the historic house.

East Meadow farmers, including the Hoeffners, were mostly "market" or "truck" farmers, regularly taking their goods by mule, horse and later motor vehicle to the Wallabout Market to sell to New York City customers. The market was located at the site of the current Brooklyn Navy Yard on Wallabout Bay. Like with many other farmers of the Hempstead Plains area, the Hoeffner crop included an ample amount of potatoes. Throughout the years, Andrew P. Hoeffner Sr. worked between 8 and 150 acres. In good times, he rented part of the Barnum property to increase his yield and profits.

The Hoeffner property was important to civic functions within the prewar community. East Meadow Hall, used for social and political functions and strongly connected to the Methodist Episcopal church across the street, sat on the southern edge of their lands. This building had been the 1868 schoolhouse when it was located up Newbridge Avenue at Front Street. East Meadow Hall opened on Labor Day in 1896 with a grand celebration featuring bicycle, sack and running races; Chinese lanterns; and decorated homes. The commissioner of the board was Richard Lowden. By the 1950s, the Hoeffner family members had turned to construction with their ACE

Hoeffner Farm, circa 1919. *Hoeffner family.*

One of the most iconic photographs of "early" East Meadow is of a hunting party posing in front of the East Meadow Hotel during the Hoeffner years. *Raymond Hoeffner.*

Steck Homestead. *Hoeffner family.*

(Andrew, Clifford, Edward) Hoeffner Contracting Company, and the property was used to store materials for their projects. The family built the East Meadow Post Office on the southern edge of their property in 1952, just north of East Meadow Hall, and leased the land to the federal government. Previously, mail would be delivered by Rural Free Delivery from Hempstead and Hicksville (once a day beginning in 1905, thanks to Richard Lowden's efforts in expanding postal service to rural East Meadow). The branch was technically an extension of the Hempstead Post Office until 2001.

The hotel building began falling into disrepair. In 1962, Clifford Hoeffner, now fully engaged in the contracting business with his brothers, looked to dispose of the hotel. He offered it to the East Meadow Union Free School District, if the trustees agreed not to tear down the historic building. Seeing educational value in the property, school district officials considered the offer, but legal experts advised against the transaction. That October, Hoeffner offered to give away the house (and $500 in cash!) to anybody willing to move the old building and preserve it as a museum. Ultimately, the Town of Hempstead took the land by eminent domain in 1963, and the building was moved to the Old Bethpage Village Restoration, where it serves root beer to many schoolchildren as "Noon Inn," reminiscent of 1850s East Meadow. Veterans Memorial Park (Prospect Pool) was built in its stead.

The Hoeffners were close to their neighbors, Charles and Emma Steck and John and Anna Moskowski, and their extended families. The Steck Homestead was razed in 1952 to build Meadow Dairy. Moskowski rose to prominence as an athletic coach. Dr. Raymond Hoeffner Jr. still owns a home in East Meadow and has been instrumental in the preservation and of local history and the furtherance of genealogical research.

THE CURIOUS CASE OF THE CARVED CENTENARIAN

How old is John Lubetsky? Who is his wife? Why are they really in court? These were just some of the questions surrounding the odd case of *Lubetsky v. Lubetsky* in the fall of 1916.

On August 11, 1916, East Meadow couple John and Pauline Lubetsky got into a heated domestic argument. Shortly thereafter, and for unknown reasons, John was declared insane and admitted to Kings Park Hospital. After his discharge as sane a short time later, Lubetsky made the spat with his wife known and alerted local authorities. According to Lubetsky, "She grabbed a knife and dug it into my wrist." He had his wife arrested on September 12, and the case came before Justice of the Peace Walter Jones of Hempstead. Justice Jones attempted to have the two reconcile their differences, but John insisted that the case proceed to trial. The next court date would be October 27. Meanwhile, John went to live with one of his sons, William; Pauline went to live with a daughter, Anna Olish.

By the time of the court case, John Lubetsky had become something of a local curiosity. It was widely believed that he was 110 years old. His wife was believed to be between 86 and 90. (Having been born in Poland in an era without accurate records, their exact birthdays were unknown.) The two elderly residents had been married nearly 60 years, apparently in peace.

When the case came to court in October, Pauline Lubetsky was charged with assault with a dangerous weapon. John, who listened to the proceedings with his hands cupped behind his ears, was hoping for a quick jury trial. It was not to be—a lawyer was absent, and although a jury would be selected the following week, the case would continue in December. A most unusual discussion ensued following their appearance in the courtroom, however—one that would shroud the case in mystery. Lincoln Haskin, John Lubetsky's attorney, claimed that his client's wife was a young woman of twenty-five or twenty-eight years old. He believed they had been married a few years. The entire case, he said, stemmed from jealousy of a younger man. H. Willard Griffiths, the defendant's attorney, insisted that his client was ninety years old and that the younger woman in question was the couple's daughter. His other children, most of whom lived in and around East Meadow, were called to testify. There was a huge range in the ages of their children, who were mainly working as tenant farmers.

At the trial in December, the identity of the "real" Mrs. Lubetsky was again in question. Haskin finally admitted that he was mistaken and that the alleged twenty-eight-year-old was, in fact, Lubetsky's daughter. He refused to believe, however, that Pauline was ninety-one years old. Haskin insisted that the woman was John's second wife and could not be more than fifty. Either way, Haskin seemed to be terrible at guessing one's age! John Lubetsky Jr., sixty-three, a key witness in the case, did not appear in court. When he could not be found, the jury was temporarily dismissed. Seemingly having had enough of the charade, John Lubetesky Sr. asked his young-looking ninety-one-year-old sweetheart if she would like to end the quarrel and return home. According to news accounts, the two left the courtroom arm in arm and walked down Front Street. Hopefully they put away the carving knives.

Part II

COMMUNITY ORGANIZATION

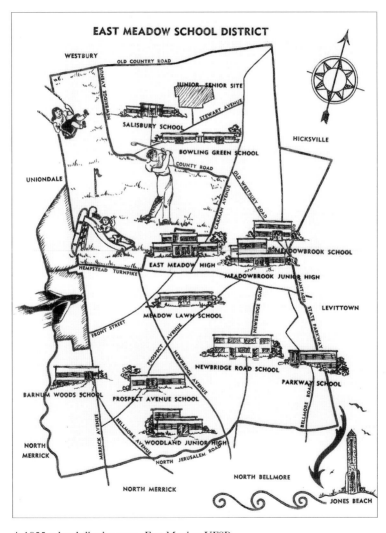

A 1955 school district map. *East Meadow UFSD.*

EARLY EMERGENCY RESPONSE

The earliest residents of East Meadow did not have fire protection. Most of the buildings were far enough apart that if one burned down, others would be spared. Fires, while unfortunate, were part of life on the Hempstead Plains. East Meadow's most prominent property owner, P.C. Barnum, was not immune simply due to his wealth. His large new barn was struck by lightning and consumed by fire in July 1885, resulting in a $5,000 loss.

Large Gilded Age estates at the turn of the century had some fire protection through Uniondale's Meadow Brook Hook and Ladder. As East Meadow grew into a more suburban community, its active residents saw the need for such a service and took it upon themselves to organize a Firemen's Association in 1921. Fire (Benevolent) Hall was erected on Maple Avenue in 1922, and two volunteer companies worked to protect residents. A used fire truck was purchased by Frederick Bickmeyer, who donated it to the community and stored it in his garage on Glenmore Avenue.

On February 2, 1930, the East Meadow Fire District officially formed. The first five commissioners were Bickmeyer, Martin Marcinkowski, William Maitland, William Lowden and Louis Schneider. Trucks were stored at the homes of volunteer firefighters, and alarms were sounded by hitting iron hoops on Prospect Avenue and Roslyn Place with sledgehammers. The few installed hydrants were connected to local wells and did not provide much

Original fire truck. *Nassau County Archives.*

EMFD Station No. 2. *Hoeffner family.*

pressure. A simple white structure with two garage bays and a modern alarm system was constructed soon thereafter at Newbridge and Park Avenues. By 1936, it was deemed too small for adequate operations, but voters would not approve the construction of a new headquarters until 1947. At that time, the main building was erected next to Front Street School. Enlarged several times, it still serves the district. The old Station No. 2 house at Park Avenue was replaced in 1972 with a modern brick building that is still in operation.

The baby boom era brought thousands of new structures to East Meadow, largely a result of the Levittown development within its borders. William Levitt donated land on which a new station would be built, with the stipulation that the department quickly construct a building for fire protection. Since voters were reluctant to approve a permanent building until 1959, the department purchased a surplus army Quonset hut and converted it to Station No. 3. This station, now a modern structure, is located on Newbridge Road. A large bond issue passed in 1951 added Station No. 4 to the Salisbury area on Carman Avenue and enabled the department to add several modern trucks and communication systems. Call boxes were added

Station No. 1. *East Meadow Fire District.*

on East Meadow streets, and children were instructed how to use boxes to sound the alarm. Perhaps the most important development of 1951 was the creation of the East Meadow Water District. This district eliminated wells from residents' yards while ensuring the availability of powerful and reliable sources of water for fighting fires.

Meadowbrook Hospital opened as a two-hundred-bed county facility in July 1935 after four years of planning and construction. Considering it was built during the height of the Great Depression, the amount of money spent on the land and buildings—$1.9 million—was enormous. The hospital mainly served the rural population of mid–Nassau County and treated fewer than 150 patients per day. To support their care, a relatively large staff of 330 was employed.

The main building faced Hempstead Turnpike and was architecturally significant, featuring a solarium on the west and east sides designed by Eggers & Higgins. A major expansion in 1950 resulted in a large complex of buildings behind and next to the original structure. Further expansion occurred the following decade. Many of these buildings can be seen today from Carman Avenue.

Meadowbrook Hospital became Nassau County Medical Center in 1970 and embarked on a tremendous building project. While still under

Meadowbrook Hospital, 1946. *Gottscho-Schleisner Collection, Library of Congress.*

construction that July, the new tower suffered a setback: a financially devastating fire in the tar roof of a four-story section of the new building scorched the steel and brick construction, melted aluminum panels and broke windows, which prompted an evacuation of Meadowbrook Hospital's other buildings. The Dynamic Care Building opened in February 1974 at a cost of $49 million. At nineteen stories, the building quickly became the tallest in Nassau County.

PUBLIC SCHOOL ON FRONT STREET

East Meadow School District is among the oldest in New York State and has been continually educating students for more than two hundred years. First conceived in 1812, when the state's Common School Act established a system of public schools, and reorganized when that law was amended in 1814, Common School District No. 3 of the town of Hempstead was known as Brushy Plains and, soon after, East Meadow. This numerical designation continues today. According to unverified oral histories, the original one-room schoolhouse was located at the northwest corner of Front Street and East Meadow Avenue. Maps from the antebellum period, however, show the school diagonally across the street, where three more buildings would serve the community's children until 1950. The original structure may simply have been moved after it was no longer useful as a school.

School funding was a mixture of state aid, local tax revenue and tuition (known as "rate bills"). Tuition was waived for families who could not pay and was eliminated completely in 1849. Throughout the nineteenth century, this rudimentary school educated the farm children of the rural hamlet—generally fewer than one hundred students per year. The district borders were almost the same as they are today (though, for a time, included the North Merrick area), so one can imagine how long it took some of the children to get to school if they lived near the Bellmore or Westbury borders. The schoolhouse bell, which beckoned these youngsters to class, survives to this day at the public library!

The earliest teacher described in historical records (though certainly not the district's first) was Carman Cornelius (1821–1893). Cornelius was born in East Meadow and, though deprived of a continuous education himself, obtained a teaching certificate before running its school in 1837 and 1838. His parents, Benjamin and Ruth (Darby) Cornelius, resided on a farm on Newbridge Road near today's Hampton Street. After a stint teaching in the Jerusalem School (District No. 5), Carman moved to Roslyn and worked with his brother Charles to become a blacksmith. He eventually returned to take over his parents' farm. He married fellow East Meadow resident Phebe Jane Combs in 1845 and was drafted into service during the Civil War. From 1865 to 1871, Cornelius rose to prominence and became supervisor for the Town of Hempstead. In this role in 1869, Cornelius authorized the sale of the Hempstead Common Lands to Alexander Turney Stewart. Cornelius's parents lived with his family on the homestead, which expanded across the road and was worth more than $10,000. After leaving East Meadow for the Freeport in 1874, he served as deputy treasurer of Queens County and finally as the first president of the newly incorporated village of Freeport in 1893. While engaged in civic work, Cornelius was in the conveyance and insurance business. His son Albert followed in Cornelius's footsteps and served as Queens County assistant district attorney.

Carman Cornelius.

The first schoolhouse was old and inadequate, and land was purchased to expand the grounds and erect a new building. In 1868, a new school was built on the property that is still owned by the district and now houses the East Meadow Public Library. The first building was overcrowded as soon as it was built, complicated further by a compulsory school attendance law in 1874. The law threatened to commit "habitual truants" between ages eight and fourteen to the "Town Poor House," a notion that certainly got reluctant kids out of bed and into the classroom. It took years for district residents to approve funding for a two-room school, which was finally constructed in 1895. A $3,000 bond issue financed the entire project. The 1868 schoolhouse was sold for $41 and taken by horse to the Schultze property, currently the East Meadow Post Office parking lot, and used through the 1960s as East Meadow Hall.

Some teachers enforced discipline quite strictly, but in 1882, the teacher Andrew Foote was himself disciplined for use of corporal punishment on one of his pupils. He resigned that June and was replaced by Reverend F.M. Hallock. Mr. Foote had been a prominent teacher in East Meadow, and he

The 1868 public school (moved). *East Meadow UFSD.*

helped organize the South Side Teachers' Association in 1880. The longest-serving teacher of that era was Miss Marie Powers (1872–1935), who was born in East Meadow and educated the community's children for more than forty-four years, from around 1888 through June 1933. (It was common for rural schools in the nineteenth century to hire girls who had just graduated. Mrs. Hull was the more experienced teacher with whom she originally worked.) Miss Powers certainly made a statement in East Meadow—she was known for driving a bright-red car, which she was able to purchase on her $400 annual salary.

After only fifteen years of use, the 1895 two-room frame structure was deemed inadequate for East Meadow's children. Truthfully, the building was never big enough, but the taxpayers of the late nineteenth century were not known for their enthusiasm spending money on public education. They occasionally splurged on entertainment, such as bringing impersonator Charles Bloomer to school in 1907. Children participated in assemblies in the little school, which balanced scholarship awards with humorous readings. Little Mia Powers brought down the house in 1888 when she sang "How a Jealous Husband Was Conquered" at the winter concert.

The 1895 public school.

Professor W.F. Hill of Gloversville City, New York, was appointed principal in the summer of 1896. Hill was a talented musician, and the district purchased a $100 organ for his use with the children in the new school. The district paid Hill $600 annually to perform the duties of school custodian and librarian as well as teacher. Perhaps these conditions led to high turnover in the next few years, although rural school districts often employed a new teacher every year or two. Harrison Williams served as principal and librarian for the 1897–98 school year, overseen by trustee Henry Fream. Fream, along with tax collector George Wood, Treasurer George Fish and Clerk Frank Tatem, were the equivalent of today's board of education. The yearly budget was $1,500. In 1900, Gerald Foster became principal, followed soon thereafter by Fred Smith. James Reese served as principal from 1903 to 1905, before he moved to South Carolina to become a professor of education at Benedict College. The district had a hard time filling his position because of a lack of housing in East Meadow. By 1908, the principal was A.H. Chubbuck.

In August 1911, a beautiful "modern" $17,000 brick building replaced the two-room schoolhouse, which was bursting with more than one hundred pupils. The builder of the 1895 school, Elbert Smith, purchased wood back from the district. The new school had four classrooms and was graded: typically, two grades were taught together by one teacher. It was designed by Hempstead architect Isaac Baylis, designer of the larger Washington Street School in Hempstead. Although East Meadow's structure no longer exists, it is possible to see a nearly identical building in nearby West Hempstead: Chestnut Street School (constructed in 1913 after the 1911 establishment of that district). The 1911–12 budget for educating seventy students in East Meadow was $4,825. Peter Hansen Berg Jr. (1866–1934) was the school trustee most credited with campaigning for the new school. Berg, who was born, raised on and subsequently ran a large farm at the southeast corner of Front Street and Merrick Avenue, served for six years.

There were some opportunities for field trips and sports. For instance, in the years prior to World War I, children competed in the county fair at Mineola. Principal J.E. Davis organized the East Meadow Athletic Association in 1917, with Henry Bickmeyer and Herbert Tatem in charge of the organization. An endearing custom was to pick flowers every June and create large daisy chains to decorate the eighth-grade graduation ceremony. Having no high school of its own, East Meadow's students mostly attended Hempstead High School.

The 1911 public school. *Nassau County Archives.*

After World War I, developers built homes near Stuyvesant Avenue, and the school-age population experienced a mini "boom," although East Meadow was still primarily agrarian. Front Street School, as it became known, was expanded to meet the needs of a growing community. Four additional classrooms and a basement were built in a large annex on the rear of the building. The 1922 extension had offices for the principal and board of education trustees and featured modern bathrooms and heating. The same year, electric service came to Front Street and illuminated its classrooms, designed for such use for the first time.

For the next three decades, Front Street School typically employed one teacher per grade, with some combined classes. Payroll and attendance records show that the average salary in the 1920s was $1,500 per year (about $22,000 in 2022 dollars, adjusted for inflation). Through World War II, class sizes ranged from about fifteen to twenty-five.

The 2020 coronavirus pandemic, which shuttered schools nationwide for months, was not the first time East Meadow schoolchildren were forced to sit home to avoid spreading disease. A June 1900 localized measles outbreak and October 1913 rash of scarlet fever caused weeklong closures

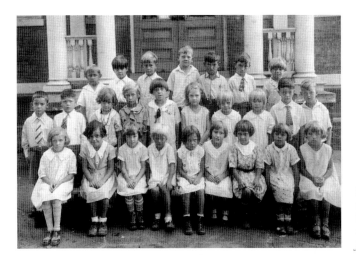

Schoolchildren at the new Front Street public school. *Hoeffner family.*

in the district. In September 1942, it was not disease but rather agricultural demands that caused the district to open a week late.

The Common School Act of 1812 did not allow for permanently hired teachers. Yearly, the district's trustee(s) would find a suitable teacher and create a contract laying out terms of employment, often featuring housing arrangements. In East Meadow, the practice of boarding teachers was revived much later than one would expect. There was a relatively stable period beginning in the 1880s when teachers would return year after year, although the 1910 federal census shows Miss Lora Harwood boarding with Peter Berg Jr., who was influential in school affairs. Then came the postwar baby boom. After the Kostynick family built a home on Green Avenue, single women schoolteachers recruited from colleges by the district superintendent would rent rooms upstairs from 1951 to 1962. State law changed, and districts could hire teachers on tenure-track appointments without finding new employees every year.

KEEPING UP WITH THE JONESES' CHILDREN

The area of the most significant development following World War I was off Newbridge Road. When that neighborhood's school opened to children east of Newbridge Avenue in 1928, classes took places on the first floor while the second floor was still under construction. Initially, students used the basement to play and ate lunch at their desks. The district's student population reached 366 when the Newbridge Road School was fully ready for use in late 1929. Land on which the school was built was donated by a prominent resident, newspaper editor Arthur Brisbane. Brisbane accepted $3,500 for the property but returned the money to pay for elaborate new playgrounds at both district schools. The money was donated in memory of his brother-in-law and fellow East Meadow resident Trumbull Cary. Between the two world wars, when East Meadow was still a sleepy rural hamlet, the school population stabilized, and 400 to 500 students were enrolled each year in District No. 3. Schools were modernized and upgraded to include conveniences such as electricity and telephone service.

Through the Depression and war years, each building educated students from grades one through eight, with one teacher per grade in each school. Both Front Street School (Public School No. 1) and Newbridge Road School (Public School No. 2) were overseen by a single principal, Allen S. Davis (originally of Cape Vincent, New York). Frank E. Church became the longtime supervising principal in 1932. He had previously served in that role in Island Park. When his annual salary was increased in 1937 to $3,500, Board of Education president Raymond Fish said, "I have been a member of the board of education for 15 years, and Mr. Church is by far the best principal we have ever had during my time." Students had more innovative opportunities than in the past, with extracurricular clubs, instrumental music classes (by 1933) and organized

The Newbridge Road school, after additions.

Principal Frank Church, 1939.
Author's collection.

physical education classes (beginning in 1939). Under teacher and coach Charles Noble, boys learned sports such as boxing and wrestling, and girls learned to dance. Marie Powers, now near the end of her impressive career, ran the 4-H agricultural club. Movies were shown in both buildings after the school day. Classes were offered to immigrants seeking American citizenship. That program also administered the literacy tests required to vote, still legal at the time. A school certificate showing completion of at least the eighth grade exempted new voters from such tests. East Meadow was part of the shared second supervisory district led by Wellington C. Mepham. Before each school district grew large enough to hire individual superintendents—beginning in East Meadow with Edward McCleary in 1953—Mepham oversaw all the common schools in a section of Nassau County.

The first hint at future growing pains in East Meadow schools occurred in 1932, when the district's 421 students briefly exceeded the district's capacity, and one class was learning part time. Wellington Mepham, superintendent of the second supervisory district, found it difficult to hire new teachers; perhaps the ongoing economic depression made it difficult to obtain the requisite education and experience. Additionally, attendance in East Meadow was exemplary, with the district praised for its 97 percent attendance rate—the highest in the supervisory district in 1933.

In 1940, the president of the board of education was James Donahue, who was active in local Republican politics. Throughout many demographic changes, Republican politicians maintained either direct or indirect control over school affairs, choosing and influencing school leaders and engaging in patronage representative of town and county affairs.

Explosive population growth following World War II resulted in double sessions in 1948. The district purchased several lots for future schools, but taxpayers were hesitant to spend so much money on new buildings. A $900,000 school supported by the Parent-Teacher Association and William Lowden, president of the board of education, was soundly rejected by voters that year after the East Meadow Civic Association, essentially a conservative organization, launched a campaign against it.

Trustees began planning for East Meadow's first high school, which required voters to approve a change in district type. Since 1812, East Meadow operated as a common school district, which is only authorized to educate students through grade eight. The district paid tuition for students who wanted to continue their secondary education in a village with a high school. Schools were overseen by Harry Gross, superintendent of the second supervisory district, which included other common school districts in the town of Hempstead. In April 1948, East Meadow became a union free school district, which would allow it to eventually operate an "academic department" (high school grades). This change was necessary because Hempstead Union Free School District No. 1, which had taken in East Meadow's high school students for generations, grew rapidly in the years immediately following World War II. Hempstead's trustees informed East Meadow's leaders that Hempstead High School would soon no longer be able to accommodate out-of-district students. After a five-year transition, East Meadow pulled out of the second supervisory district. Most common school districts in the town of Hempstead changed to union free school districts during the same period, even if they did not operate their own high schools. The change would allow them to expand their boards of education to five or seven members and hire their own superintendents. Technically, a "union" school district means that two or more common districts could combine their territories as one, but in practice, neighboring districts never consolidated. Local control was, and continues to be, a defining factor in Long Island schools.

During the 1945–46 school year, there were 467 students enrolled in two schools. This number represents typical enrollment for the two decades prior to and including the Second World War. Three years later, as the first Levitt homes were built in East Meadow, the number grew significantly to 798. By 1951, when Lakeville Estates was opening, the enrollment ballooned to 2,774. Three years later, when myriad housing developments were completed (forming the vast majority of homes found today in East Meadow), total student enrollment was 10,033. This would only increase through the 1960s as the Greatest Generation parents sought greener pastures for their baby boomer children when they became school age.

The district ran out of space in 1947 when one hundred children from Veterans Emergency Housing Project at Santini Sub-Base enrolled and overwhelmed the schools. The program converted former army barracks into 184 apartments, 20 percent for Mitchel Field veterans. All available space was used to try to accommodate students, including a locker room and custodial rooms. Island Trees and Jerusalem (Levittown), themselves operating in ancient facilities overwhelmed with runaway population growth, had been sending some students to East Meadow on a tuition basis. The practice ended with the entry of children from Santini. To complicate matters, the children came from tax-exempt government property, and the district needed to raise funds from other residents to support their education. Adam Kurpisz, an official of the East Meadow Taxpayers Association, ran for school board in opposition to the Veterans Emergency Housing project, arguing that the veterans' children were getting a "free ride" on the backs of taxpayers. In 1950, a further influx of children from the Santini housing project burdened the district's finances, and the board of education took legal action against the state for payment of those students' educational costs. They were supported by other districts with public or military housing (e.g., Long Beach) who faced similar situations.

The first of the modern structures, all of which were designed by architect Frederic Wiedersum, was the twelve-classroom Prospect Avenue School. (Some of Wiedersum's five hundred Long Island schools are nearly identical, including original sections of East Meadow High School, Wantagh High School and Merrick Avenue Junior High School.) Board president William Schindel broke ground in May 1949, and Prospect was occupied in September 1950. That October, the board mulled adding ten additional classrooms to Front Street School to handle the rapidly growing new entrants.

Less than two months later—December 5, 1950—just as Long Island was experiencing the largest "baby boom" in American history, a spectacular fire destroyed the Front Street School, which was deemed to be beyond repair. Newspaper articles from the following day show gleeful children proclaiming their freedom from education, but their joy was short-lived. The district scrambled to place 635 students in temporary spaces: the partitioned Prospect Avenue School gymnasium, the firehouse and the Republican Club. Students were taught in triple sessions for three hours per day. Kindergarten, introduced just four years earlier, was suspended until 1952 while the district planned a multimillion-dollar expansion project. Outraged parents demanded a rapid construction program. The board focused on quick construction of Meadow Lawn School and expansion of Prospect Avenue School. An addition to Prospect doubled its size one year after opening. Expanded yet again in 1954, it could accommodate 960 children at a construction cost of $1,194,149. Frank Church was its instructional leader until 1967.

Opposite: Constructing Prospect Avenue School. *East Meadow UFSD.*

Above: Meadow Lawn School, 1951. *East Meadow UFSD.*

District officials decided that the Front Street property was not large enough to handle a modern school plant, so they concentrated on quickly completing a planned school just several blocks away on Devon Street. Taxpayers had already approved the purchase of a school site on a newer residential grid northwest of Prospect Avenue. At the time, the new numbered streets cut through mostly open fields. Original plans called for a two-story secondary school at a cost of $950,000, but it was defeated by taxpayers. A smaller $650,000 building was approved in 1949. The original design included space for both elementary and secondary pupils, with the idea that the building could be used as a high school in the future. As the district finalized its plan for purchasing a high school site and constructing a suitable building, officials prepared to welcome students in kindergarten through grade nine at Meadow Lawn School. Front Street School teacher Robert Wiebel served as Meadow Lawn's principal until 1976.

Before the new school opened, the Committee of East Meadow Citizens worked closely with parent groups and the board of education, convincing their neighbors to approve an addition to the building. This wing would double the size of the school before initial construction was completed.

Workers rushed to finish their projects, and Meadow Lawn School opened to students in September 1951. The cost for accommodating up to 960 elementary and junior high students was $1,265,000. That same month, the district purchased a site on Carman Avenue for the future high school. Board members and administrators then turned their attention to the massive expansion program that would add eight additional school buildings by 1955.

With the opening of military housing facilities at Mitchel Manor and Santini Sub-Base, additional students came to learn at Meadow Lawn. Programming for both children and adults was expanded throughout the decade. In 1969, Meadow Lawn was renamed George H. McVey Elementary School in honor of the influential educator who oversaw enormous growth of East Meadow schools during the 1950s. McVey, who started as a science teacher in Queens, was on the board of education from 1948 to 1958. George McVey Jr. fondly remembers his father running to the Front Street School fire in 1950 and throwing important school records from the burning edifice to firemen below. In 1958, McVey was hired to become assistant superintendent, a role he had for ten years. In 1969, just prior to his retirement, McVey was the acting superintendent. He died in 2003. McVey remains one of the largest elementary schools in East Meadow.

Bowling Green School opened on Stewart Avenue in 1952 and was doubled one year later by taking the plans and creating a mirror image extension to the west known as Bowling Green II. The total cost for the two connected buildings was $2,629,722. Built to accommodate 1,920 children—initially through junior high—it is currently the largest and most attended elementary school building in the district. School population in the district exploded to 6,475 in 1953. Newbridge Road School was expanded in both 1952 and 1954, adding classrooms, a gymnasium and cafeteria and making it the district's largest elementary school (costing $1,327,149 to construct).

Barnum Woods School, built on May Lane on the old Barnum estate, was occupied in 1954 for 960 students at a cost of $1,327,222. Although planned in 1951 as a combination elementary/junior high like Meadow Lawn and Bowling Green, it was never utilized as such. It was the first school in five years to have single-session classes, but only because grades four through six were temporarily housed at the new Woodland Junior High School when it opened on Wenwood Drive the following year. Still, Barnum Woods's construction, funded largely ($1,025,222.50) by the U.S. government due to children attending from nearby Mitchel Manor, significantly alleviated

Meadow Lawn sixth-grade class, 1951–52. *East Meadow UFSD.*

Bowling Green under construction, 1952. *East Meadow UFSD.*

Left: The "key" to Barnum Woods, 1954. *East Meadow UFSD.*

Below: Bowling Green principals, 1954. *East Meadow UFSD.*

crowding in the district. The rear wing was expanded a year later, and a four-classroom extension at that junction was built in the mid-1980s. Barnum Woods became known for its high socioeconomic factors. Involved families there have overwhelmingly represented the district in leadership positions and participated in governance affairs. School leadership has been remarkably stable, with only three permanent principals (Joseph Romano, Peter Valente and Gregory Bottari) since its inception.

The climax of school construction in East Meadow was 1955, with a total of six buildings opening, beginning in January with East Meadow High School. Administrators Samuel "Red" Manarel and Dr. Alfred Sellers, both previously of Bowling Green, led the new school. Manarel had launched freshman sports teams in 1954, when EMHS had a soft opening with eighth- and ninth-grade classes. Salisbury, Parkway and Meadowbrook Elementary Schools started in April; Woodland and Meadowbrook (later McCleary) Junior High Schools opened in September. Three secondary schools' total cost was $8,758,212. Elementary schools were reorganized for K–6. Meadowbrook Elementary, Parkway and Salisbury each opened for six hundred students at a cost of $842,298 per school. All three were expanded within a few short years: the front of Meadowbrook School, the side of Parkway School and the rear of Salisbury School. Former National Football League star and Fordham Rams coach Ed Danowski set up the new junior high athletic programs.

W. Tresper Clarke Junior-Senior High School opened on district's north side in 1957, the first in the county to offer a full program in technical trades. Its gymnasium was the largest in the county. East Meadow High School gained a permanent wing in 1959, then a still-utilized temporary wing four years later. Students had staggered attendance times to accommodate the crowd. Peak enrollment in East Meadow schools was approximately nineteen thousand students in 1963–64, when the district was headed by Edward McCleary. It was then the most populous school system on Long Island and the third-largest non-city district in the state. The baby boom generation brought modern programs in guidance, special education, the arts, vocational and adult education, although taxpayers disapproved of a swimming pool proposition. Experimental Acceleration Program allowed gifted students to complete grades four through six in two years. The Nassau County Jail School partnership for educating inmates began in 1963.

All in all, the district spent more than $20 million in 1950s dollars on its modern construction program, which is the equivalent to over $200 million today. It is easy to imagine how much stress school board trustees were under

Immunizations at school, circa 1954. *East Meadow UFSD.*

to keep budgets in check, finance construction projects through bonds and hire enough faculty and staff members to keep the district running. The East Meadow Public Library opened on the Front Street School site in 1960.

East Meadow was not known for extravagant spending. In 1966, the district budgeted one dollar per student for educational communications, which put it in the 15th percentile. There were many record players in East Meadow's schools, perhaps a testament to the outstanding music department for which the district has long been acclaimed. Both music and sports brought enormous pride; marching bands won parade ribbons year after year, and coaches led the East Meadow Jets and Clarke Rams to numerous division and state championships.

The 1970s and 1980s saw central leadership by Martin Walsh and Frank Saracino. Declining enrollment brought several years of failed initial budgets and disagreements over school closings.

Originally called "the oval school" on architectural plans, Salisbury School was built on the old Ladenburg racetrack as the surroundings transformed into sprawling subdivisions, dotted with the occasional remains of Gilded

Junior high art class, 1950s. *East Meadow UFSD.*

Age estates. Within walking distance to the Conservative synagogue and a highly ranked school, northwestern Salisbury became predominantly Jewish and relatively affluent compared to other sections of the district. With a more educated populace came smaller family sizes, more involved parent-teacher associations and a reputation of having a small private-like school dubbed "the country club." It was prestigious to live above the "Mason-Dixon Line"—that is, Hempstead Turnpike.

The student population of Salisbury School peaked at about 1,100 very soon after the building opened. As with Meadow Lawn School on the south side of the district, an additional wing was constructed soon after the original building was occupied. As the baby boom waned, the school suffered a large drop in population. By 1971, there were only 470 students, and at its lowest point in 1973, only 291 learners filled spaces that were available for up to 960. Conversely, the secondary schools were experiencing the effects of overpopulation now that the children born in the '50s were growing up. One of the first proposals to solve both problems involved moving the administrative offices to a wing of Salisbury, thus maximizing available space and freeing up classrooms at East Meadow High School. About 250 parents, seeing school closures ahead, protested the plan. A similar plan for Bowling Green School was rejected by the school board later that year after 900 parents packed a meeting in opposition because it would have involved busing children to other neighborhoods.

Norman Labelson moved to Birchwood in 1972 so his children could attend Salisbury. He walked into an ugly debate. "They called us the 'Cadillac Crowd,'" Labelson recalled, "because we lived in brick splits." The Bowling Green parents, typically blue-collar Christians, used this term to mean *Jews*—and not in a kind way. The school board, controlled by the latter faction, did a poor job masking anti-Semitism behind certain decisions. They sought to close Salisbury for cost-cutting reasons, but board president and conservative faction leader Bea Bryson thought that busing Salisbury children to Bowling Green would help them "see how the other half lives." (Prospect Avenue parents, faced with similar circumstances two years later, pushed for a JCC at their school, should it close. The board quickly dismissed the idea.) There were many protests in the spring of 1973, involving hundreds of people outside buildings and inside board meetings. On April 5, Chester Tuchman, attorney for 216 Salisbury parents, presented board president Michael Meyer with legal documents taking the case to State Supreme Court in June. Days later, in the early morning, Salisbury fathers picketed outside the home of Superintendent (and former Salisbury principal) Martin Walsh, while mothers and children lined up outside East Meadow High School, then his office, demanding he keep the elementary school open. Tuchman lost the case, which centered on the religious divide. He argued that the board had been "arbitrary and capricious" in closing Salisbury and that it purposely pitted the Newbridge Road and Salisbury school zone parents against each other. Justice Daniel Albert believed that the financial needs of a united community drove the board's decision and noted that "no evidence was called to the court's attention to substantiate [anti-Semitism], and it is thus disregarded as without merit."

About 300 Salisbury children transferred to Bowling Green in September 1973, bringing enrollment there to 1,450. The district leased Salisbury to Nassau BOCES, which used the building as its headquarters for more than two decades. An interesting result of the highly publicized controversy was the fomentation of a discussion of privilege and integration. Over time, the neighborhood lost its character as a Jewish enclave. Salisbury is now home to district offices.

Salisbury protest,
1973. *Jim O'Rourke,
from* Newsday.

Burton Scholl was elected to the board of education for the 1974–75 school year to fill a vacancy. According to Scholl, a few issues caused so much division that the board met eighty-three times in one year. These three issues were a teachers' strike; a proposal to extend the Learning Center, a controversial program in which elementary students made contracts with their teachers; and, of course, closing school buildings. A committee was commissioned to study which school should be closed, and Prospect was the recommendation. The study technicians thought that it would see the fewest repercussions. According to Scholl, Bea Bryson ("a very conservative, staid, refined lady") was "very quick to subscribe to the advocacy of the technical report" and that more attention was paid to the terrible coffee at executive sessions than this decision. Since Scholl lived in the neighborhood, he became the "defender of Prospect." He did not believe that the evidence was compelling and intimated to fellow board members that he would make a statement of opposition in public. Scholl called the board's actions "irresponsible and reprehensible," explaining that the schools Bryson and her allies chose to close were illogical—political vendettas or socioeconomic divisions were more important than choosing the oldest building, the one with declining enrollment or the one with the highest resale value. He was successful in convincing two members, Anthony Falanga and Angelo Gaglione, that another study or analysis was warranted. The board at its

March 24, 1975 meeting voted four to three that Prospect be closed. To assuage the feelings of the people in the Prospect community, somebody suggested that Newbridge Road School should also be closed in a "King Solomon decision" so that Prospect was not being targeted. Public outcry and multiple demonstrations led by Ruth Kramer of the Committee for Quality Education delayed the inevitable one year. The Committee and Lakeville Estates Civic Association unsuccessfully sued the district to prevent Prospect's closure. They campaigned against the 1975–76 budget and successfully elected new trustees Harvey Weintraub and Elaine O'Sullivan, who led the board in reversing the closure that summer.

Prospect and Newbridge nevertheless closed in 1976 in the wake of serious budgetary problem. That year, the district was on "austerity" and imposed fees for non-essential supplies, including diplomas. McCleary's doors were shuttered in 1982 and, like Prospect, was knocked down for housing development. Newbridge was converted to apartments, its auditorium serving for a short time as a dinner theater. New wings were later constructed at Woodland and Clarke to make way for new students from these homes. The district alleviated crowding in its elementary schools by transitioning to a 6–8 middle school and 9–12 high school configuration in 1990. A contract dispute lingered so long that year that elementary teachers vowed to prohibit birthday parties until they received raises.

Financial woes plagued the district in the early 2000s, leading to conflict between the teachers' union and administration. In a notable protest, popular longtime elementary teacher Richard Santer faced disciplinary action while participating in a union-sponsored picket in front of Woodland Middle School. District officials charged that Santer and others, though legally parked, had been unsafely blocking traffic during student dropoff. Bond issues financed critical early 2000s upgrades, but school leadership did not undertake a major infrastructure construction project until the passage of a $60 million bond in 2017 that included reconstruction and expansion of the East Meadow Public Library. Aside from physical plant improvements, significant funding for arts and athletics were included, showing the district's dedication to those disciplines.

The status of kindergarten was a thirty-two-year saga. East Meadow was one of the last districts in the state to continue a half-day program. As early as 1983, Shelly Domash led working parents on a crusade for all-day instruction. Under President Michael Turner, the school board put a budget referendum to the voters, who rejected the notion. Major parent involvement over issues of early childhood and state testing mandates emerged in 2014. Social media groups called Parents for Full-Day Kindergarten (led by Stacy Rosenfeld-VanWagenen, Tara Fitzpatrick and Wanda Small) and East Meadow Opt Out (led by Ilene Ballato and Alicia Piazza-Coffey) unified to fundamentally change the district's leadership and install board members who would chart a new direction. Under future board leader Alisa Baroukh, 75 percent of Barnum Woods parents refused to allow their children to take state assessments linked to unpopular Common Core curricula. The district followed a "sit and stare" procedure for students whose parents refused standardized tests. Full-day kindergarten began in 2015, immediately after Superintendent Louis DeAngelo departed. Within four years, the old bloc was voted out, and Dr. Kenneth Card was installed as superintendent. Educator Scott Eckers and attorney Matthew Melnick were the first leaders under the new majority, which consisted principally of younger parents. School closures and restrictions due to the COVID-19 pandemic created a hostile environment for the board of education in 2021 as angry parents flooded meetings protesting health regulations and diversity initiatives imposed by state and county departments.

WHO WAS W. TRESPER CLARKE?

Arjun Panickssery, W. Tresper Clarke High School class of 2020 salutatorian, contacted me asking about the namesake of his school. He had seen conflicting information about the initial "W": was it William or Walter? Several sources, including my last book, show Tresper's son William with the suffix "Junior," but did the "W" stand for William… or was the "Jr." an error? Knowing that the younger Clarke was in the first East Meadow High School marching band, I contacted William Katz, well-known local music teacher and director of that band. Mr. Katz's memory at age ninety was impressive: Katz was able to recall the names and professions of almost every student in a 1957 photograph. Unfortunately, he did not have the answers we sought, and Arjun and I turned to available records.

Walter Tresper Clarke was born on May 13, 1905, in Columbus, Georgia, to parents Kate Matthews and Walter Robert Clarke. He had two younger siblings, Julia Ellen and Robert Vincent. According to census records, all three Clarke children were known by their middle names as early as infancy. "Tresper" studied engineering chemistry at the Georgia School of

Technology (now Georgia Institute of Technology) before graduating in 1927. At school, he was active with the Emerson Chemical Society.

Clarke married Mary Louise Snodgrass in Brooklyn, New York, in 1936 and had two sons, William and Robert. Mary Louise had been a schoolteacher in her native Florida. The Clarkes lived on Washington Avenue in Brooklyn while Tresper used his professional skills as chief chemist for Rockwood and Company, a chocolate and cocoa manufacturer just down the street. In 1943, Clarke and two coworkers obtained a U.S. patent for the invention of a soluble cocoa product. In other words, they advanced the science of creating cold chocolate milk in which the cocoa does not quickly settle.

During World War II, Clarke moved his family to Rockville Centre. At the war's end, the Clarkes moved to 826 Preston Road in East Meadow. From May to September 1945, Clarke worked for the Technical Industrial Intelligence Committee, a U.S. Army agency. He went to war-torn Germany after V-E Day with a group of scientists and engineers with the goal of studying the German wartime factory system to exploit its advancements for the free world. Clarke, a food chemist, brought back intelligence on the German food industry, specifically surrounding specialized production and distribution during the war that could be used to improve civilian and military applications. For this patriotic service, First Army commander Lieutenant General Willis Crittenberger honored Clarke in 1951.

Following the war, Clarke was a regular author in *Candy Industry*, a scholarly journal. At first, he published articles about his visits to the German factories, focusing on descriptions of machinery, manufacture of cocoa powder, government control of cocoa bean distribution and specialized recipes for delicacies such as marzipan. He expanded into more scientific pursuits, such as the use of microbin and abacterin in the chemical process of making and preserving chocolate. In the 1950s, Clarke researched and authored articles on all things chocolate—avoiding cacao product abuses, controlling flavor and color by particle size, keeping liquid chocolate in a fluid state and successfully delivering it in bulk. He detailed historic Mayan and Dutch processes for its manufacture.

W. Tresper Clarke became involved with the East Meadow Taxpayers Association, or Independent Taxpayers of East Meadow (ITEM), a conservative organization that dominated local politics in the postwar years. He penned a letter to *Newsday* in 1948 encouraging district residents to "study, understand, [and] act" instead of jumping to conclusions from hearsay and other secondhand sources. Clarke was elected to the board of education in 1948 and served as its president from 1950 to 1954. During that time,

W. Tresper Clarke. *East Meadow UFSD.*

he became involved with the local Protective League, a nativist, pro-business and anti-Communist society that grew out of World War I anti-German vigilance committees. It was through these organizations that W. Tresper Clarke made his alliances and achieved domination over local affairs. Clarke and his team made many controversial decisions through one of the most tumultuous eras in East Meadow's history. These involve Red Scare "witch hunts" of perceived rivals, active promotion of school prayer, showing supposed preference for hiring teachers aligned with his own religious and cultural beliefs and allegedly involving himself with corruption regarding the awarding of bids and the selection of the district's politically connected attorney. With the friendship of George McVey and other notable leaders, Clarke and the board of education transformed and modernized East Meadow's schools. The district became the largest in Nassau County. As president, Clarke oversaw the massive, rapid construction initiative that built every school building currently in use and several more that have now been closed.

Mary Louise Clarke died at age forty-eight in 1956. She had been a children's librarian for the New York Public Library and the Freeport Memorial Library. Her most memorable accomplishment was the compilation of East Meadow's first known history pamphlet, *East Meadow: Its History, Our Heritage* (1952).

After his wife's death, Tresper moved to Toronto, Canada, married Mildred Redmond and continued to work for various companies as a chocolate chemist. In 1962, he received the Stroud Jordan Award for his contributions to the field of confectionery technology. Although Clarke only lived in East Meadow for ten years, his influence was so strong that trustees named the district's second high school after him in 1957. W. Tresper Clarke came back to East Meadow for the school's formal dedication later that school year. In the first yearbook (*Scope*, 1959), he wrote to students and said that their "increasing knowledge of the arts, sciences, and humanities brings all of us greater hope for peace, happiness, world tolerance, and dignity among all nations." Clarke was "humble and proud to have been one of the many who helped to project and carry out

W. Tresper Clarke Junior-Senior High School. *East Meadow UFSD.*

plans for your education which today bear such splendid dividends and which will grow to maturity." Coming out of retirement in the late 1970s, Clarke invented the chocolate/peanut butter center of Reece's Pieces. He died in 1987 in Arlington, Texas, and was buried in Riverdale Cemetery in his native Columbus, Georgia.

The 1957 East Meadow High School yearbook, *Résumé*, features William Tresper Clarke Jr. Aside from his involvement in band and the boys' athletic association, the yearbook indicates that the young Clarke was interested in following his father's footsteps in becoming a chemical engineer. It is unclear how Clarke continued at East Meadow High School after his father moved to Canada.

So, the "W"? Through the magic of the internet, I was able to track down W.T. Clarke's grandson Christopher Clarke. He initially thought that the initial stood for William, since his little brother is William. His father, however, confirmed that the "W" does indeed stand for Walter. Case closed!

POSTWAR POLITICAL FACTIONS AND THE PETE SEEGER SAGA

As East Meadow began transforming into a modern district in April 1948, the growth of its school system provided a breeding ground for partisan interference and ideological influence. These issues were largely us-versus-them disputes related to control, patronage, religion and money. Socioeconomic factors heavily predicted group membership.

East Meadow Republican Club was organized in about 1931 by Walter Lowden and William Maitland, with Edward Dougherty becoming president. When its membership exploded to more than three hundred in 1932, the club met at the East Meadow Fire Hall and then at East Meadow Hall before opening its tax-exempt clubhouse in a former store just north of Newbridge Road School in June 1936. The clubhouse, remodeled and expanded in 1957 and demolished in 1981, hosted local political functions but also served as a private social club of sorts, complete with a bar. At its founding, the club drew heavily from residents of Irish and Italian heritage.

The factions that dominated the East Meadow political scene for two decades were Independent Taxpayers of East Meadow (ITEM) and the Committee for Better Schools (CBS). ITEM, which incorporated as an official organization in September 1962, grew out of the Protective League membership from the 1940s and 1950s. The Protective League's chairman in the 1950s was attorney (and later Senator) Edward Speno, who promoted "business…men and civic leaders." ITEM was headed by John Curry. CBS grew out of a group known as The Coalition, a looser organization established in 1954 as the Good Government Group (GGG). On paper, these were committees comprising concerned citizens who wanted to control the educational system. Each was headed by a chairman who held meetings and put up a slate of candidates each year. Leaders' children, now senior citizens, spoke of meetings taking place in their living rooms and basements.

ITEM was not known for its independence. Robert Kushner, local activist heavily involved with school efforts in the 1960s and later six-term school board member, recalled that "ITEM enjoyed a symbiotic relationship with the Republican Party." The organization was supported by the East Meadow Republican Club and furthered conservative social viewpoints, worked to reduce taxes by tightly controlling or limiting school physical and programmatic expansion efforts and chose school leaders who were sympathetic with their causes. Principals and superintendents, often businessmen first and educators second, were chosen by school boards that were controlled year after year by the Protective League and ITEM. They rewarded loyalty to the cause by naming school buildings after their standard bearers (such as when Edward McCleary retired in 1969).

In 1952, Richard Halstead, trustee and former president of the Lakeville Estates Civic Association, and Coleman Parsons, leader of the board's three-to-four minority faction, highlighted supposed discriminatory hiring practices within the district. In a year when the district's four schools (Newbridge,

Bowling Green, Meadow Lawn and Prospect) needed to hire ninety teachers, officials struggled with hiring experienced and highly qualified educators. Not one Black teacher was hired, the progressives noted, although New York City's most prominent education programs had many Black graduates. There seemed to be few Jewish teachers, he observed, although Jews constituted a considerable percentage of graduates of prominent education programs. Halstead thought that it was the duty of the board to investigate whether racial or religious prejudice existed and wished to examine hiring practices and conduct a survey of existing staff members. McCleary denied hiring teachers with regard to race, religion or political affiliation because "the law doesn't permit me to inquire" and noted that Harry Gross, second Supervisory District superintendent, had to also approve candidates. Parsons conducted exit surveys of departing teachers and noted alleged violations of civil rights laws. Some teachers spoke of religious discrimination under McCleary and Principal Frank Church. Church asked about religion, on the supposed grounds that he would need to hire substitutes for holidays. "An inquiry was made about my religion by Mr. Church," one teacher wrote, "to discover whether I was a Jew." Another wrote, "During the two years in which I served at East Meadow, I did not encounter any obvious displays of political, religious or racial prejudice. When I was hired, I was asked by the interviewer if I belonged to a specific religious group. The questions stirred within me intellectual and emotional reaction regarding the administrative policies of the East Meadow System."

Parsons pivoted to a business manager search and asked Albert Silver, previously a candidate for such position, to give whistleblower-type testimony. Forrest Willits conducted interviews; Silver testified that "there was no real discussion during this interview on any fact of procurement, accounting or finance....The most vital question asked was relative to the clubs or organizations of which I was a member." The community learned that the Republican Club doled out jobs for the district. Applicants were expected to bypass the official process and see Tom Hennessy at the club, who would then meet with McCleary, supervising principal for the entire district, and find unfilled positions. McVey would typically approve the appointments.

Committee for Better Schools was not officially supported by any political party, but its members were known as the community's liberals. "Coalition" members supported school budgets "with a concentration on student needs" that raised funds for additional classrooms and progressive school programs such as the 1970s "learning centers." They spoke in favor of local artistic and educational pursuits that were controversial in postwar suburbia and were typically supported by the teachers' union. The group's membership tended to reflect the makeup of East Meadow's most heavily Jewish neighborhoods and drew significantly from the Barnum Woods, Prospect and Salisbury zones. CBS accused ITEM of putting religious and political interests before educational ones but could not garner enough support to take a majority of trustee seats. Catholics, who initially faced discrimination when moving to Protestant-majority East Meadow, found themselves migrating to ITEM over religious and social issues. With the Knights of Columbus, St. Raphael Church's leadership strongly advocated for its members to elect ITEM candidates who would presumably be in favor of Catholic moral tenets in schools, as well as the preservation of tax-supported busing to parish schools. ITEM went further. A member tried to prevent former resident and First Lady Eleanor Roosevelt from speaking at a Salisbury PTA meeting because she would be "controversial." Board president Edward Moss issued a clarification related to fundraising legalities…and a new invitation, which Roosevelt rejected. Reverend Frederick Lerner's widely distributed pamphlet, *It Could Happen in East Meadow*, was considered anti-CBS propaganda linked to opposition over a Planned Parenthood presentation. By the 1970s, the divide seemed tribal: music and gifted programs for the "Cadillac crowd" versus football and tax breaks for hardworking laborers. In 1971, half of the district's twelve PTA units tried to secede from PTA Council because Marjorie Rosen, a candidate for president of that organization, supported a ticket called Taxpayers to Improve Education. Norma Gonsalves, Republican leader of the traditional majority, warned PTA leaders to remain nonpartisan. She went on to become a civic leader and presiding officer of the Nassau County legislature. Her nephew and finance manager Joseph Parisi became school board president decades later.

In 1952, the school board's majority faction, under W. Tresper Clarke's guidance, was accused by three taxpayers and the board's Coalition minority of wasting public funds to illegally and improperly hire John Borrie as the school's general and project attorney. The district was in the middle of a $12 million expansion project, and Borrie's opponents alleged that the board majority granted a contract giving the lawyer excessive funds for the length of the project—up to ten years—even though 1,600 residents signed a petition voicing opposition to the contract. The minority faction wanted to hire a lawyer yearly and pay that person a flat retainer plus a fee for extra work performed, rather than the arrangement that had been in place, which paid the attorney 0.5 percent of the planned work plus a flat fee per year. In 1952, that salary's base was $60,000—the equivalent of about $584,000 in 2022! Clarke was challenged in the state's Department of Education in Albany but was found to ultimately have authority to enter into a contract with the attorney of his choice. Borrie would stay on in this role for many years, representing the district when it was the respondent in its most famous case, *East Meadow Community Concerts Association v. Board of Education of Union Free School District No. 3*.

In 1954, the newly formed GGG accused trustees W. Tresper Clarke and Forrest Willits of "raiding our pocketbooks, disgraceful partisan politics, tricky and cynical real estate deals and plain garden variety stupidity." Parsons had earlier accused the board majority of keeping students on double- and triple-session classes instead of quickly addressing overcrowding. Clarke decried the charges as "ridiculous," but Nassau County district attorney Frank Gulotta opened an investigation into corruption; the Coalition members offered evidence. The board majority sent an official letter to all households arguing its side, but the GGG quickly attacked them for using public funds to promote the Protective League. The case was short-lived due to threat of a libel suit, but Willits decided to finish up his term and not run again, citing personal business. Clarke completed his term and moved away from East Meadow. McVey stepped down from the board in 1958 and was immediately hired by his friends to become the district's assistant superintendent.

East Meadow Community Concerts (EMCC) was a nonprofit organization that brought performances to the community for ten years. In 1965, its president, Norman Novak, applied to use the auditorium at Clarke High School, as was customary, to present a series of concerts the following year. Among the selections was folk singer Pete Seeger, who was to perform on March 12, 1966. The application was approved with no issues; it was not until after an October 23, 1965 concert in Moscow that Superintendent Edward McCleary or the school board became aware of a potential problem: Seeger had sung anti–Vietnam War protest songs in Russia. One month later, the conservative board led by ITEM-backed Owen Walsh met and voted to cancel the concert out of fear that "the people in our community would be enraged" as it would invite controversy and stir up protest. In an injunction hearing, district counsel John Borrie said that if Seeger "sang nothing but folk songs like 'Old Black Joe' there would have been no controversy." He took issue with the singer's left-wing sympathies, arguing that school property needed protection and that the Knights of Columbus, Veterans of Foreign Wars and American Legion were opposed to the event. In 1955, Seeger famously refused to answer questions from the House Un-American Activities Committee about his earlier involvement with Communism, leading to a conviction that was later overturned. (A year prior, Bowling Green School recalled rented trumpets because they were made in East Germany.)

Novak and his organization sued the school district in Nassau County Supreme Court in February 1966; Judge Edward Robinson Jr. said that nobody's rights had been violated. He pointed to the district's regulation that "the Board of Education reserves the right to show cause and revoke any permission granted to an organization when in the best interests of the school district it deems it necessary to do so." The case went immediately to the Appellate Division, which agreed that EMCC's constitutional right to free speech and assembly were illegally restricted but dismissed the case as moot because the concert date had passed. Meanwhile, the district allowed a speaker from the conservative John Birch Society to speak to students, a move highly criticized by Bill Nelson and the East Meadow Citizens' Committee, which supported the concert.

Novak's attorneys, including Norman Bard and next EMCC president Samuel Millman, appealed to the New York State Court of Appeals in June, arguing constitutional grounds and involving the American Civil Liberties Union. Millman had earlier taken issue with Borrie's "Old Black Joe" comment, fearful of censoring and blacklisting. In appeals court, Justice Stanley Fuld opined that "the expression of controversial and unpopular views…is precisely what is protected by both the Federal and State Constitutions." Essentially, schools can bar all outside organizations from using facilities, but if they allow groups to use the facilities, they cannot selectively choose which to allow based on viewpoint. They can ban events that are illegal or pose a threat, but the Seeger concert was neither. Fuld enjoyed a lengthy and significant career as a celebrated justice; the case has long been cited as precedent. The only dissenting justice, John Scileppi, championed conservative, pro-Catholic causes reflective of East Meadow's ITEM majority.

The district appealed again in January 1967 but lost in a 6-1 decision authored by Fuld. The district was ordered to host the concert March 8. Almost a year after the original date, Seeger performed to 1,100 fans, with more than 300 protestors outside (organized by the American Legion under Joe Sorok). Notably, Seeger's first song was the national anthem. Millman became a state assemblyman, and Bard became board of education president. EMCC continued presenting concerts at Clarke—without incident—for several years.

ITEM, which opposed Seeger's performance, used the situation to influence board elections—Walsh was reelected. But the "pressure group" showed its first crack. Herbert Auerbach, two-term ITEM trustee with four years as president, broke ranks and denounced the group as having excessive influence in school decisions. Realistically, it would have been difficult for any Jew to be part of ITEM by 1967. The group only thinly veiled its anti-Semitism and adopted the term "Cadillac Crowd" as a plausibly deniable slur. Rabbi Charles Kroloff, member of Clergy and Laymen Concerned About Vietnam and leader of Community Reform Temple, which moved from Westbury to Salisbury after merging with Temple Beth Avodah in 1974, slammed the district's concert prohibition. His sermon the week of the canceled event reminded congregants to take action against injustice: "I do not believe that tranquility is a primary goal of our society." Auerbach lost his seat. Millman, who ran on the CBS line, was defeated after ITEM leadership launched a smear campaign linking him to Seeger.

The issue of school prayer was first raised in 1949 by several local districts. At that time, W. Tresper Clarke, incoming board president, chose to adopt a "wait and see" approach to the decision. A rabbi spoke against the proposal, and several local reverends spoke in favor of it. In 1953, the Protective League, headed by George McVey, sought to "improve the moral and spiritual welfare of the children" by encouraging prayer each day. He proudly proclaimed his opposition to progressive education. McVey was opposed by Coalition leader Coleman Parsons, future president of the East Meadow Levitt Home Owners Association; Richard Halstead; and Nahman Zirinsky. By May, the school board majority had created a media blitz

EAST MEADOW COMMUNITY CONCERTS ASS'N.

Presents

Pete Seeger

At The

W. TRESPER CLARKE HIGH SCHOOL

Wednesday Evening, March 8th, 1967
8:30 P. M.

Admission by this ticket only

American Legion protest at Clarke. *Luckey, from* Newsday.

East Meadow High School, 1955. *East Meadow UFSD.*

accusing Dr. Parsons of being a Communist because he had previously obtained insurance from the International Workers Order. Parsons went so far to ask the Federal Bureau of Investigation to investigate him to prove his loyalty.

The events surrounding that election, which prompted a record 7,500 residents to register to vote, caused the creation of the GGG the following year. The Protective League used Red Scare tactics in 1955 to defeat GGG candidates Henriette Janke and Mark Lessing. In 1956, the League, working together with the American Legion (run by attorney W. Timothy Darrah), opposed GGG candidates and came under fire for distributing literature that read, "Once again the Good Government Group is backing members of subversive organizations" because candidate John Gebhardt was a member of the New York City Teachers Union. Gebhardt sued the League and its president, Robert Mannion, for $150,000 for libel and for pressuring independent candidates to withdraw from the race. The Supreme Court's 1962 *Engel v. Vitale* decision prohibiting school-sponsored prayer rendered East Meadow's decision moot. Nevertheless, ITEM-backed trustees refused to change the policy manual and had school leaders recite, "We will now commence a moment of silence to enable those individuals who wish to ask God's blessing on this day's activities to do so in accordance with their own beliefs." These daily moments continued until 1983.

GOLDBLATT'S SAND PIT

Joseph Goldblatt's East Hempstead Sand and Gravel Corporation began operations on Newbridge Avenue in 1927, its business centering on the mining and sale of minerals. By the end of the first year, his sand pit had breached the water table and covered 20.2 acres with an average depth of twenty-five feet. At some points, water depth reached more than forty feet. Mining continued beneath the water table, and the corporation used property across the street for general operations and storage. In 1931, Goldblatt changed the company name to East Meadow Realty Corporation and modernized with the developing "transit mix" industry. By the following year, the corporation was engaging in cement mix operations, which required large trucks to enter and exit the property. The name was later changed to Builders Sand and Gravel, under which Goldblatt and his son Herbert operated through numerous legal challenges after the Town of Hempstead passed updated zoning laws. Joseph died in December 1954. Herbert took over Builders Sand and Gravel and his father's other business, Heroes Excavating and Contracting Company.

Goldblatt and seven officers of six other corporations were indicted under charges of price fixing in April 1939. The allegations were that the companies conspired to rig prices on sand sold to Nassau County for Works Progress Administration (WPA) projects (at $1.25 per yard) and orchestrated strikes of workers at firms who did not participate in the scheme. The defendants pleaded not guilty. After a two-week trial that June, the jury found all the defendants not guilty.

The Town of Hempstead passed Ordinance No. 16 in 1945, prohibiting mining in residential neighborhoods. In 1956, State Supreme Court justice L. Barron Hill permitted Herbert Goldblatt to continue his "nonconforming" operations because the business began before the ordinance was enacted. In May 1958, homeowners who lived near the sand pit appeared at a town Zoning Board of Appeals meeting to prevent Goldblatt from continuing a cement mix operation, which they claimed polluted their homes with particulate matter. Interestingly, the homeowners' attorney was State Senator Edward Speno, who advocated using the land for a park. This park, later constructed, was named in his honor.

Goldblatt ran into further trouble in 1958 when the Town of Hempstead amended Ordinance No. 16, which prevented disruption to the water table by prohibiting underwater dredging. Goldblatt was ordered to fill in the mine, which he estimated would cost him $1 million. He refused to comply,

The Sand Pit, 1953, looking southeast. *Steve Buczak Archive.*

even after losing on appeal. The town also enacted a series of more stringent requirements surrounding fences, retaining walls and slope of the mine. In June 1959, the Town of Hempstead again attempted to shut down Goldblatt's business over violation of these ordinances. Goldblatt argued that the town took no such action against nearby mining operations and was therefore discriminating against his business. A case against the town reached the Court of Appeals of the State of New York. In *Town of Hempstead v. Goldblatt* (1961), Justice J. Burke wrote the majority opinion affirming the lower court's ruling that the ordinance was constitutional. Justice J. Van Voorhis, writing the dissenting opinion, argued that violations had been corrected, the pit was safe and the Goldblatts had invested heavily in improving the property. He felt that the town's ordinance was directed squarely at Goldblatt.

Throughout these cases, Goldblatt and his attorney, Edward Miller, believed that the town would eventually obtain the property. They thought the town authorities were continually challenging the viability of the business in attempts to devalue the land prior to condemnation. Goldblatt also claimed that local authorities were violating his Fourteenth Amendment due process rights because he was unable to earn a living from property he owned. Meanwhile, the sand pit continued as a popular hangout spot for neighborhood families, who used the manmade lake for swimming in the summer and ice skating in the winter.

Ice skating on the frozen pit, circa 1929. *Steve Buczak Archive.*

At the time, flooded sandpits had come under intense scrutiny in Nassau County, with newspapers publishing stories about how they attracted mischievous youngsters and contributed to accidents. On a Saturday night in August 1944, Richard Gerlach, a sixteen-year-old visiting his friend, drowned while swimming in the pit. Three summers later, fourteen-year-old Alfred Steenhuizen nearly drowned before being heroically rescued by his friend Hartley French. Complying with an ordinance, Goldblatt built fences with barbed wire, making the sand pit safer. Walter Lowden, from one of the oldest families in East Meadow, remembers that parents warned their children not to go to the "forbidden" sand pit. Many youngsters swam instead in the East Meadow Brook, a shallow stream on the Barnum property known as the "BAB" or Best American Beach.

A lawsuit against the town (*Goldblatt v. Town of Hempstead*) reached the U.S. Supreme Court in 1962. Justice Tom Clark wrote the court's unanimous decision that the town ordinance was constitutional even if it deprived Goldblatt of his property or the ability to run his business. According to the high court, it was reasonable for the Town of Hempstead to exercise its police power to shut down what they believed to be a danger. Clark opined, "If this ordinance is otherwise a valid exercise of the town's police powers, the fact that it deprives the property of its most beneficial use does not render it unconstitutional." The court did note, however, that it was difficult to ascertain the reasonableness of some of the regulations. It also questioned the prohibition of further excavation below the water table. Although Goldblatt was ordered to backfill the pit, further developments did not make that necessary.

In 1963, the Town of Hempstead Board embarked on an ambitious project to expand parkland within the town's borders. After voting in March to acquire the Hoeffner property for the purpose of constructing a park and swimming pool at Prospect Avenue, the board voted on April 23 to purchase eighteen acres of Goldblatt's sand pit to build the future Speno Park. The remaining twenty acres of Goldblatt's property was obtained by Nassau County for water drainage. It was to be acquired through eminent domain, and both parcels were condemned that year for public acquisition. Goldblatt, who was already embroiled in a dispute over local zoning and use of his sand pit, valued the land at $1,815,000, saying that he would have developed the property. The issue at hand was the ease of filling in the sand pit to make the land flat enough to construct either public works projects, such as a hospital, or individual housing lots. Following a four-year legal dispute with town and county administrations, who valued the land at a combined price of $245,000, State Supreme Court judge Howard Hogan awarded Goldblatt a total of $507,795.

After years of setbacks, eighteen acres taken by the town in 1963 were finally developed into Speno Park. When it opened in October 1989, the new park had taken twelve years of planning and construction at a cost of more than $2.5 million. The remnants of the sand pit have been incorporated into a county storm basin north of the park. In 1997, the artificial lake and surrounding property was transformed into a nature preserve and bird sanctuary, off limits to the general public and maintained by Nassau County and the Council of East Meadow Community Organizations (CEMCO). Trees in this unique East Meadow location have since matured, creating an unlikely oasis in the middle of dense suburban development. The idea of a wildlife sanctuary was first voiced by Edmund Trunk in 1963.

Local organizations such as Kiwanis Club help CEMCO clean up the preserve twice a year, and Eagle Scout projects have studied environmental impact through science classes, documented its history, cleared trails and improved the sanctuary through the construction of bat boxes, which help control the mosquito population. Other projects by Troops 469 and 362 include the construction of bird, owl and wood duck nesting boxes, the creation of a "bug hotel" and mason bee houses, planting a pollinator and Long Island Little Bluestem native prairie grasses and building shelters for amphibians, reptiles and fish. These individuals and groups have helped restore a sense of East Meadow's rural landscape in a place where the land itself had been ravaged, giving it a much brighter future.

MITCHEL FIELD

Long a center for innovation and experimentation in air and space travel, the Hempstead Plains were home to both military and civilian airports. Mitchel Air Force Base, also known as Mitchel Field, was part of a larger aerodrome system that included Camp Mills (training center) and Hazelhurst (later Roosevelt) Field. By 1917, these facilities were providing training and transportation for American soldiers departing to fight in the Great War raging across Europe. The base was originally Hazelhurst Field No. 2 but was renamed for former New York City mayor John Mitchel, who had recently lost his bid for reelection and decided to serve his country by joining the war effort. He died in Louisiana in 1918 during a military training flight. Following the war, Camp Mills was incorporated into Mitchel Air Force Base, located just to its east.

Mitchel Field matured between the two world wars. The military added barracks, hangars, warehouses, offices and recreational club facilities. The base expanded into the property that once served as the Meadow Brook Club and Cold Stream Golf Course. East Meadow's growth was partially tied to the growth of Mitchel Field: barracks and military housing grew at the Santini Sub-Base (near Glenn Curtiss Boulevard) and Mitchel Manor (constructed in 1950). Santini housed the all-Black 2244th Aviation Engineering Squadron, deactivated in December 1949. The years during and directly following World War II were busy times for military personnel in East Meadow. New Cantonment Hospital at Santini Sub-Base treated wounded soldiers returning from overseas, and the base hosted the Red Cross, a theater, chapel, post office and numerous shops. When the Meadowbrook Parkway extension was completed in 1956, Santini was cut in half, and a bridge was built over the parkway to connect the two sides. This "bridge to nowhere" still exists at Kellenberg Memorial High School.

As Mitchel served as a major training center, experimental flights were common at the field. In 1939, a two-engine Lockheed XP-38 fighter piloted by Ben Kelsey crashed while attempting to land at Mitchel Air Force Base. The plane was part of a secret program to build the fastest and most modern aircraft. Further airplane crashes in East Meadow in 1943, 1948 and 1955 mobilized certain residents against the airfield. Mitchel was decommissioned as an active Air Force Base in 1961.

On the afternoon of November 2, 1955, a B-26 bomber crashed into Paul, Susan and Susie Koroluck's lawn at 61 Barbara Drive, killing pilots Charles Slater (of East Meadow) and Clayton Elwood and miraculously

"Bomber Crashes in Street," by George Mattson, 1955. *The Pulitzer Prizes.*

missing residents playing and walking on the dense Salisbury Park Manor street. Mothers and children, most of whom were home at the time, vividly remember the loud noises and shaking buildings. Eyewitnesses claimed to have seen the pilots waving at them to warn of impending disaster, from which the Smith, Spatz and Cohane families narrowly escaped. Panicked parents rushed to collect their children, while the fire department quickly responded. A photograph that George Mattson took from another plane won the Pulitzer Prize. The Korolucks were housed at Mitchel Field while air force contractors repaired their fire-damaged home. They were able to move back by April.

In another tragic incident, a small airplane unrelated to Mitchel Field experienced engine trouble and crashed into a Prospect Avenue home on November 10, 1961. In the crash and explosive fire that ensued, the pilot and an eighteen-month-old child were killed before twenty-seven eyewitnesses.

Today, the majority of Mitchel Field is the North Campus of Hofstra University and Nassau Coliseum. The diagonal driveway and parking lot on Hofstra's North Campus is the remains of a runway, remnants of which also exist in the brushy plains on the campus of Nassau Community College. Santini Sub-Base is home to residential, educational and recreational facilities. Mitchel Manor still hosts military families.

HISTORIC CHURCHES

Religious organizations have played an important part in the social history of East Meadow since its earliest days as a rural community. The oldest in East Meadow is the Methodist Episcopal Church, whose old frame structure on East Meadow Avenue now houses a newer congregation. The church was the largest and most influential religious organization in the United States throughout the late 1700s through the early 1900s. East Meadow's congregation was organized in 1857 by Peter Lewis, David Sprague, John S. Smith, Joseph Smith and Parmonus Post. The following year, the Noon family (of the East Meadow Hotel) donated a plot of land, and the building was constructed. A parsonage was built by Samuel Powers in 1891, supported in part by George Mott, Esq. The original church burned and was replaced with the present structure in 1897. The congregation moved across the street to its parsonage property in 1953. An annex was built six years later.

For several generations, the Methodist Episcopal church was the center of religious life in East Meadow. Its members were typically also trustees and leaders of the school board, town political clubs and the closely connected East Meadow Hall. Though influential, East Meadow did not always have a permanent preacher. In the 1880s, East Meadow, Uniondale and Foster's Meadow (a German farming community in the Elmont area with many

Horse-drawn sleigh at church, 1904. *Mary Louise Clarke Archive, East Meadow UFSD.*

The Methodist Episcopal church. *Gary Hammond.*

George Mott. *R.G. Clarke.*

ties to East Meadow families) all shared the same pastor. In the spring of 1885, the churches quarreled over service times and payments to the proposed minister; East Meadow had two services a day, while Uniondale contributed more money.

An interesting ecclesiastic argument occurred in 1893 when George Mott, prominent attorney, wanted to donate a sizable number of books to the church's Sunday school library. Reverend Platt did not want to accept the donation because Mott was not a church member and did not live his life in line with church teachings (he was thrice married). Nevertheless, Mott had supported church functions in the past, and most members wanted to accept his charity. At the end of the debate, the church board unanimously voted to receive the books.

At the turn of the century, Reverend Robert Wodehouse led the church. Reverend Harry Hofstadt took over after Wodehouse left for a journey to Africa. In 1908, Methodist Conference leaders assigned Pastor Oscar Buck to the East Meadow congregation. The Methodist Episcopal Church was not always tolerant toward religious minority groups. In February 1870, for example, members of the church forcefully broke up a Mormon church meeting, ordering them to leave and threatening them if they continued to attempt to convert their wives and daughters. Much later, Reverend David Parker was instrumental in forming interfaith relations through the Clergy Fellowship. This association has held an interfaith Thanksgiving service yearly since 1982.

St. Francis Polish National Catholic Church was built on Harton Avenue in 1932. Father Bernard Bobek was the first priest, and services were conducted in Polish. This area of East Meadow had recently seen an uptick in its eastern European population, and Polish was a common first language of many residents. One of those residents, Rose Gniewek, organized a Women's Society. The Gnieweks owned a business around the corner on Newbridge Avenue. The baby boom era brought more congregants; a new altar was constructed in 1956, and a rectory was built one year later. A sizable Polish school operated out of St. Francis Church.

Another local church grounded in its immigrant roots is the Holy Trinity Orthodox Church on Green Avenue. Worship services in the Koshansky home began in 1918 with Priest Maxim Dzemba. Established in 1924 as the

St. Francis Church. *St. Francis Church.*

Holy Annunciation Church, it was the earliest Orthodox Christian church on Long Island. The first pastor was priest John Zawojski, and the original frame structure was located behind the current building. A planning mistake led to the church's construction on a lot next to the one the congregation purchased (which they then had to buy as well, leading to financial distress). Growth during the baby boom necessitated the construction of its present building (on the "correct" original lot) beginning in 1961, with additions through the 1970s. The church is notable for its architecture and artwork.

One of the most unusual scenes in East Meadow religious history took place in 1929, when the parishioners of the Orthodox Church quite publicly disagreed with the way Father Zawojski was handling the church's bills. Over the prior three years, Zawojski had helped to organize the religious and physical structure of the organization. The church cost about $8,000 to build, and the priest raised about $7,000 toward its construction. He wanted to assess the congregation to pay off the church's debts, while most of the members wanted to pay with regular funds. Many of them wanted him removed, and a legal fight ensued. On October 14, three hundred members stationed themselves outside the church, armed with fresh eggs. As Zawojski arrived, they pelted him until yellow liquid covered the seemingly unpopular man. As he tried to escape in his car, a woman opened the door

Left: Holy Trinity Church. *Holy Trinity Church.*

Below: St. Raphael's Church. *St. Raphael's Church.*

and continued the assault. After police arrived, three women were arrested for disorderly conduct. The pastor must have reconciled his differences with his flock, since he served in that role for another four years.

St. Raphael Parish of the Roman Catholic Church was founded in 1941. The building was originally located at Newbridge Road and Pendroy Street, with Father Charles Sullivan as the first priest. Church services were held in the rectory and an old farmhouse before an old frame church was moved from East Williston to the property in 1942. As the population boomed after World War II, St. Raphael's grew under Father Paul Connolly. A modern church was built by 1953 on a new property across the street. A large elementary school served the parish until 1992. In 2004 a new, larger church was built behind the school, and the midcentury structure was demolished.

Calvary Lutheran Church was organized in 1950 near a historically German-Lutheran neighborhood. The congregation first met in a storefront on Hempstead Turnpike and Taylor Avenue before building a large modern church there two years later. Led for thirty-two years by Reverend Herbert Kern, members were active in community charitable causes. Pastor Kern lived in East Meadow until his death in 2019 at age 102, serving as an East Meadow Fire Department chaplain for more than fifty years.

Christ Lutheran Church, built on Bellmore Avenue in 1959, became embroiled in controversy in 1977 when its pastor, Donald Smestad, began a "Jews for Jesus" Church of Jesus the Messiah, causing the American Lutheran Church to suspend the congregation from its membership. Over a decade, Smestad had led his flock toward their first-century Jewish roots by adopting Hebrew and reading from the Torah. About 800 participants joined the evening Jewish-type services, while only 150 remained for Smestad's traditional Lutheran services. Mainline Christians accused the church of "Christological subordination," and Jews were uneasy about the adoption of their symbols and possible proselytization. Smestad joined forces with "Abba" Jack Hickman's St. John's Lutheran Church in Massapequa. Under the charismatic Hickman, the group evolved into a youth-focused doomsday cult called Shoresh Yishai, which grew through 1983. Former members recall horrific psychological, sexual and economic abuse. Only its most fervent supporters continued after a 1982 exposé about Hickman's lies and sexual abuse of teenage boys. Some moved to a compound in Maine. The structure is now New Covenant Church.

CIVIC ASSOCIATIONS

In 1922, residents of the rural but growing East Meadow organized a Welfare Association that sought to address community concerns about "school facilities, fire protection, vigilant and social affairs." Meetings were held in East Meadow Hall and were quite productive: soon after its initial June meeting, members quickly influenced voters to approve a large addition to the school and the creation of a fire district. They advocated for a bus line between East Meadow and the village of Hempstead. Similar concerns were addressed a generation later. The group, numbering over one hundred strong, adopted the motto "Boost East Meadow." A social committee organized parties and Independence Day celebrations.

During the Great Depression, when East Meadow's population reached 1,560, local welfare efforts were often heralded by political clubs and charitable individuals. Dominick Tanzola, Italian immigrant and leader within the local Republican Party, moved to East Meadow in 1908 and settled in the Bellmore Park section after its subdivision was established. Tanzola was a gardener who ran a general store with his wife, Theresa, at their Sherman Avenue home, where they also raised an enormous family. In 1934, they converted a bungalow on their property to a storehouse, and through the Civil Works Administration, a New Deal agency, the Tanzolas provided food distribution to hungry neighbors burdened by economic disaster.

Emerging associations in the late 1940s worked together to push for better services such as water and schools. East Hempstead (Gardens) Estates Civic Association merged with neighboring Meadowbrook Manor Civic Association in 1948 and coordinated an effort to drive new residents to the polls to approve the district's plans for school expansion. The following year, they campaigned for school bus service and considered coordinating a parent-run carpool should they be unsuccessful. These developments were largely populated by war veterans and unionized employees, so it is no surprise that they would find ways of eagerly organizing themselves.

In the 1950s, civic or homeowners' associations ranged from loose confederations of neighbors to highly structured organizations with their own constitutions. A 1962 school policy handbook suggests the level of activity and influence within these associations. The district began providing free use of its Little Theaters to civic associations, but they were used so frequently that each association was limited to using the closest secondary school. Civic associations had committees that served various functions in the developments such as publishing a monthly newsletter, welcoming new neighbors or coordinating social events like dinner dances. Chairmen of finance, grievance, sports, youth and even picnic committees were active in building neighborly relationships. Community concerns over school issues like busing and overcrowding, quality-of-life issues such as unpopular construction projects and safety issues like traffic congestion were frequent topics at meetings. The Joseph-Martin Civic Association even met at Barnum Woods School in 1955 to discuss the effect of television on their kids (fearful that *Howdy Doody* would corrupt them with bad words such as *ain't*, *lousy* and *stinker*).

In September 1951, a group of parents living in Salisbury Park Manor petitioned the district to ask for a school bus stop near Bly Road. Residents of Klein and Teicholz's Lakeville Estates organized a civic association that later campaigned against unfavorable development of the old Mitchel Field property. Homeowners living in suburban developments built along Bellmore Road formed the East End Civic Association, which held dances and blood drives and successfully pressed for a teen canteen in 1955. Its East Meadow Canteen began holding summer dances at the East Meadow Fire House that June. The Carman Community Association's (a joint venture of Levitt homeowners) September 1969 newsletter weighed the pros and cons of high-density construction at Mitchel and picketed against the construction of a supermarket at Land Lane that December. By the 1970s, many of the original civic associations had pooled resources to create the Council of East Meadow Community Organizations (CEMCO). In 1989, the Cypress Circle Civic Association, Clearmeadow Civic Association and Flower Streets Civic Association, in coordination with CEMCO, petitioned to fill an unsafe sump.

Some associations are still active today, although they are largely run by only one or two residents without the assistance of a functioning board or regular elections. Infrequent meetings may occur to negotiate a shared oil or sidewalk contract, plan a block party or try to influence local politicians. Gone are the days of the monthly newsletter, but some associations are finding new life on social media platforms.

In January 2020, in a scene reminiscent of *Leave It to Beaver* or *Father Knows Best* but adapted to twenty-first-century society, the grateful denizens of Mail Route no. 30 sent off their longtime carrier, Kim Hollar, into retirement with good wishes, gifts and a surprise party organized by Susan Marks and Lois Quinn, community leaders from Wenwood Oaks. A post about the event on Todd Weinstein's "Nice Things that Happen in East Meadow" social media page garnered hundreds of likes and many personal stories of Kim over the years, even from people who didn't live on her route.

Early East Meadow telephones, connected manually, were serviced by operators in Hempstead, Wantagh and Hicksville. After 1948, "Ma Bell" modernized to the standard 2L+5N system, and customers could now dial subscribers in most local exchanges without speaking to an operator. In a blow to local identity, some of these exchange names began to change in the early 1950s. Numbers in certain combinations—including HEmpstead—were overlapping with Brooklyn numbers like GEdney and HEgeman and beginning to run out. New York Telephone introduced new exchanges with names that were easy to remember and hard to mispronounce, hence the arrival of a well-known East Meadow exchange name, IVanhoe. Direct-dial long-distance service became available in 1959.

East Meadow Telephone Exchange Names

Preserve local history and dial by letter!

22 CAstle (1)
33 EDgewood (3, 4)
48 IVanhoe (1, 3, 5, 6, 9)
73 PErshing (1, 5)
78 SUnset (1, 3, 5)
79 PYramid (1, 4, 6, 8, 9)

Created by Scott Eckers.

A socioeconomic battle of the dials played out in East Meadow when the telephone company planned to convert many HIcksville exchanges to LEvittown. According to a March 1952 *Newsday* article, "Residents living in non-Levitt homes built in Hicksville and Wantagh are supporting the East Meadow residents (living in non-Levitt homes) in their fight to stay clear of Levittown by name if not geography." East Meadow firemen and taxpayers' association members campaigned against the name, fearing the social stigma that association with recently constructed, relatively cheap neighborhoods in Levittown might bring. Enter PErshing 5 instead! Many homes near the Wantagh Parkway still use this exchange. CAstle, EDgewood, IVanhoe, PErshing, SUnset and PYramid helped East Meadow develop its own sense of identity through the 1980s.

Part III

DEVELOPMENT

Maitland Street Gang in East Hempstead Park. *Tom Carozza.*

*We at Trylon firmly believe that today's phenomenal buying is only the beginning
of an extraordinary building era, and that the American philosophy of
"a place of our own in the country" will continue to be the major force in the
demand for single family units.…The ability to own a house is present today;
the desire to own a home is becoming stronger and stronger, and the values
on Long Island continually increase.
—Ernst Heumann, 1955*

Heumann's Trylon Realty sponsored many of East Meadow's 1950s developments as the exclusive agent. His arrival from Germany in 1924, the loss of much of his family in the Holocaust, his keen business sense and his ideal location in Forest Hills led to Heumann epitomizing the American Dream of the 1950s while providing a suburban escape for American Jews.

North of Front Street

The oldest development in the Front Street area was Newbridge Gardens at Hempstead, planned by Joseph Gross in 1926. Early aerial photos of East Meadow show cleared streets in this neighborhood, which centers on Coolidge Drive. Calvin Coolidge, known informally as "Silent Cal," was president of the United States at the time of general prosperity when the development was laid out. Gross and his partners Leon Wolosoff (a supporter of Jewish philanthropism) and Morris Rosenfeld quickly built up a real estate empire on Long Island. They focused on speculative land sales rather than on home construction. Prospective builders purchased lots from them—few of them built. Max Loeb, the first owner who tried to construct a home, ended up suing the developers when he could not get electricity to his lot, something that was promised in the sales contract. In 1946, members of the Newbridge Gardens Community Association asked the town to improve their streets. Three years later, they were vocal in backing their own neighbor, Theodore Foote, in his bid to fill retiring school board trustee William Lowden's seat. Not every lot was immediately developed; midcentury residents recall seeing straight to Mitchel Field through the empty spaces. Beginning in 1950, Frank Builders Inc.'s Meadow Garden Homes project added fifty houses to the neighborhood. Salisbury Lawns added a few $16,990 split-level homes in 1953, complete with wood-paneled dining room and sunken living room.

The land for Newbridge Gardens at Hempstead came from two large parcels. The northern half was part of a series of adjacent properties owned by extroverted resident and town justice of the peace George Tatem. The southern half was land owned by F.J. Menendez and then P.C. Hendrickson. In the nineteenth century, the land was farmed by the Walker, Denton and then Turrell families. A small section of the Hendrickson property—extensions of Grant, Maurice and Albermarle Avenues—was later owned by the Ryder family and built up by Michael Forte's Adonia Homes (as Romain Homes) in 1951.

Edwin Mersereau, a prominent photographer from Manhattan's Sarony Studio, lived in a stately Merrick Avenue home, previously of B. Lewis, that

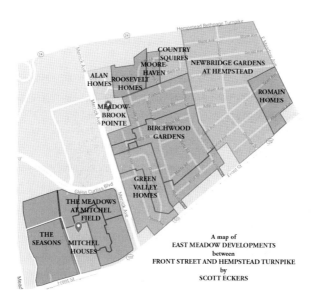

A map of
EAST MEADOW DEVELOPMENTS
between
FRONT STREET AND HEMPSTEAD TURNPIKE
by
SCOTT ECKERS

became Temple Emanu-El. Between the former David Shor and synagogue properties, one turns on Lloyd Court to enter a small development called Alan Homes, built by Morris Garelick in 1951. Moving east on Lloyd Court, one enters Roosevelt Homes, built by Julius Miller in 1960. At Rosalie Drive, Lloyd Court changes to Bard Lane and meanders eastward into a small development named Moorehaven, built by Rocco Morone in 1955. Notice that Brisbane Lane is the main thoroughfare here; the development was built at the eastern edge one of several properties owned by journalist Arthur Brisbane. Moorehaven advertised six-room "Colonial Split Ranch" houses, with modern "science" kitchens, large playrooms and garages. Sales director Edward Toner advertised the $18,490 model as "a woman's dream!" Farther east on Bard Lane is Country Squires, built by Michael Pantony in 1963 on property that once belonged to George Wood.

The entire section described in the last few paragraphs was once the homestead of Andrew Duryea and family. Moving south, a large development called Birchwood Gardens was built in three sections beginning in 1951 on the former Twersky property. The land was farmed by John Mollineux until 1868. This neighborhood is generally defined by Wickshire Drive, Norman Drive, Francis Drive, Rugby Road and Kroll Road and featured $14,290 brick capes with all-brick center halls. Steel beams allowed for future expansion, a common feature in East Meadow. Birchwood was a major player in the East Meadow development scene: its owner, Herbert Sadkin, owned Birchwood

Aerial photo of Newbridge Gardens (*bottom right*); Konta, Brisbane and old Sprague properties (*center right*); Mersereau property (*bottom left*); Santini Sub-Base (*center left*); and golf courses north of Hempstead Turnpike. *Howard Kroplick.*

Dave Shor's, run by David and Arthur Shor from 1949 to 1976. *Gary Hammond.*

Terrace Inc. Together with Seymour Sadkin and Morris Schoenfeld, the prolific builders constructed most of the homes in the Salisbury area, as well as in numerous communities across Long Island, South Florida, the District of Columbia and as far away as Kentucky. He worked with architect Stanley Klein, and together they created the "model American home" (dubbed the "Sputnik Home" for an expedition in Moscow). Sadkin, who died in 1989, was active in nonprofit organizations and became a philanthropist who supported medical research and Jewish charities.

In the southwest corner of the superblock, entering from either Peter's Gate or Peters Avenue, is Green Valley Homes. Its two sections were laid out in 1950 and 1951 around a neat circular drive. The $11,690 to $13,390 homes by J. Herbert Burmeister featured five rooms with attached garages and full basements. In typical 1950s style, sales agents Kemp and Miley advertised "colored tile baths" and the latest in electric appliances. Green Valley Homes was constructed by Edward Droesch and Ernest Amoroso on land that also once belonged to Arthur Brisbane, after being in the Turrill (or Turrell) family for much of the nineteenth century. The small section now containing a donut shop was retained by Joseph Rottkamp and is not part of the development.

Salisbury Park Manor. *Nassau County Archives.*

Most developers at the time used tree-type names to make their neighborhoods sound bucolic, regardless of the existence of actual trees. The new adjacent Nassau County Park at Salisbury (renamed Eisenhower Park in 1969) was a key selling point of Salisbury Park Manor, built by Conti Square Homes (Anthony Sagliacco, Anthony Yeni, Frank Marone and Phillip Giacondi) on the north side of Hempstead Turnpike in 1950–51. The park property was acquired from the Salisbury Golf Club's 1940 foreclosure, planned in 1944 and opened in 1949. County Executive J. Russell Sprague billed it a "People's Park for the Recreation of Generations," emphasizing its enormous size, clubhouse, sporting facilities and its Devereux Emmet–designed golf course. Salisbury Park Manor's four hundred Alwin Cassens Jr.–designed homes were planned on one hundred acres between Carman and Sprague Avenues, including much of the Carman-Lowden Homestead. The "bungalows" sold for $9,890 to $10,875. Nassau County fenced in the park in 1947 to restrict access to the golf courses. In doing so, Sprague and the remaining roads running through the park were closed.

Between Prospect Avenue and Front Street

The first recognizable suburban-type developments in East Meadow's core were that of the O.L. Schwencke Land and Investment Company. Schwencke eventually developed ten sections of Hempstead Lawns, with the first two being situated between Prospect Avenue and Front Street. He purchased the large tract belonging to the recently deceased Charles Van Nostrand (1822–1905), which was also farmed by Charles's father, Benjamin Van Nostrand (1789–1877). Land for Section 2 near Front Street was once farmed by Isaac Wright, A. Hultz and finally John Terrell. The driving force behind Schwencke's company was profit through land sales, not home construction. By the turn of that century, prices approached $1,000 per acre—an outstanding sum for the time. Hempstead Lawns Sections 1 and 2, mapped in 1908, include most of the homes situated on streets from Chestnut Avenue to East Meadow Avenue, including Glenmore, Nostrand and Belmont Avenues. In 1922, Schwencke donated land on Maple Avenue for use by the East Meadow Volunteer Firemen's Association.

Prior to the subdivision of farmland, Peter Hansen Berg owned the land at the southeast corner of Merrick Avenue and Front Street. Before the Bergs, the Lewis family farmed there. In 1925, Berg sold off much of his land (except for his home at 1606–20 Front Street) to W.D.W. Realty for the

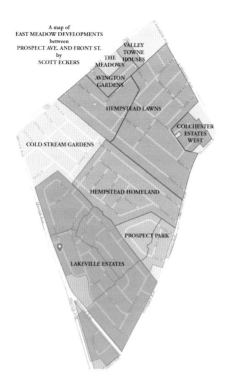

A map of
EAST MEADOW DEVELOPMENTS
between
PROSPECT AVE. AND FRONT ST.
by
SCOTT ECKERS

VALLEY
TOWNE
THE HOUSES
MEADOWS

AVINGTON
GARDENS

HEMPSTEAD LAWNS

COLCHESTER
ESTATES
WEST

COLD STREAM GARDENS

HEMPSTEAD HOMELAND

PROSPECT PARK

LAKEVILLE ESTATES

creation of Cold Stream Gardens. This area contains all the homes on Gates, Jeffrey, Berg and Green Avenues and Warren, Spring and Oswego Streets.

Cold Stream Gardens was one of the many projects of Joseph Gross (the others included Newbridge Gardens and Hempstead Homeland in East Meadow, Bowling Green Estates in Salisbury, Broadway Terrace in Hicksville and Marvin Manor in Valley Stream and Uniondale). By the end of the Roaring Twenties, Gross had acquired more than $1 million worth of real estate and moved his new publicly traded company into a six-story headquarters at 554 Atlantic Avenue, Brooklyn. Just $65 down could secure one of Gross's twenty-by-one-hundred-foot lots, and prospective customers would be taken for free to see the land. A 1927 excursion brought 1,500 interested guests in thirty-eight buses and many private cars on a tour of the properties. Individual building lots sold for $325 and up, with most houses needing three lots. Gross began to stress the investment value of his Long Island properties over the features of the homes that could be built thereupon. "YOU will make money on our Hempstead Properties," he advertised to Brooklyn customers in 1926. Proximity to the Cold Stream Golf Course (on which Meadowbrook State Parkway was extended in 1954), an expanding State Park Commission and its public beaches and the bustling village of Hempstead—a commercial, educational and entertainment center—were key points in his ads.

The most developed tract of land in this section was that of Hempstead Homeland, which was mapped in 1931 by the same corporation, Joseph M. Gross Inc. This development includes Starke, Chambers and Elmore Avenues from Prospect Avenue to Dale Avenue, plus the cross streets. Prior to its subdivision, the area near Prospect Avenue was settled by J. Smith and L. Denton in the mid-nineteenth century. P.C. Barnum later held property there, followed by Harriet Wilson in the early

Oscar Lewis Schwencke.
Napua Doolin.

twentieth century. By 1935, construction was well underway. As he did for all his real estate investment projects, Gross promised "complete city improvements" with gas, water, electric service, shade trees and paved roads and sidewalks. The 1938 aerial photograph shows houses already built on most of the lots, and a 1940 advertisement boasts eleven new homes on fifty-by-one-hundred-foot lots, complete with six rooms and a garage.

By far the largest project of the early baby boom era in East Meadow was planned and completed by Kalman Klein and David Teicholz in 1950 and 1951. The first section, located at the corner of Prospect and Bellmore Avenues, went through several name changes before development: Hyde Park Terrace, Lakeville Estates Merrick and finally Lakeville Estates (Klein and Teicholz's trademark for all their future developments in the area, based on their earlier project at Lakeville Road in New Hyde Park). Lakeville Estates was not the first project to be planned at this large property, which is generally bordered by Prospect Avenue, Spruce Lane, Cedar Lane and Merrick Avenue. The area was formerly owned by Mary Willis. In 1927, the entire section—including the triangle between Bellmore, Merrick and Prospect Avenues—was originally laid out as Hempstead Terrace Gardens. Streets were mapped on paper but never built. When Lakeville Estates was built, Klein and Teicholz transformed the previously parallel tree-named streets into suburban curves popular in the 1950s. They advertised "100 acres of parklike panorama" for "Mid-century's most luxurious and superbly styled homes," access to excellent schools (the new Prospect Avenue School) and proximity to houses of worship (i.e., a synagogue). Three different three-bedroom ranch house models (Long Islander, Contemporary and Nassau) offered every modern amenity. An "expansion garage" was available for purchase. Residents enjoyed the on-site shopping plaza, complete with a supermarket.

The small Barnum Farm Cemetery existed at Cedar Drive. Some remains were likely moved to Greenfield Cemetery by 1902, as only eight headstones remained then from the Carman, Post, Place and Williams families. According to Mary Clarke, forgotten remains were unearthed when Lakeville Estates began excavating. The cemetery may have predated the

Right: An original home in Lakeville Estates. *Doug Fehmel.*

Below: Lakeville Estates. *Doug Fehmel.*

Barnum family, since the Posts (including Jotham, who lived just south) and Carmans buried there were born in the eighteenth century and previously owned the land.

The year 1953 saw the rise of small developments near Hempstead Lawns. Avington Homes, also known as Filber Homes, was constructed by Vincent Berger and Phillip Giocondi on property owned by Peter and Grace Klein. Prior to the establishment of the Klein nursery, the rectangular property from Vincent Drive to East Meadow Avenue, including the bowling alley, was farmed in succession by Sarah Barnum, J. Van Nostrand, C. Smith and Henry (and later Edward) Alsheimer. Children would play baseball on the empty lots that constituted the former nursery. Later condominium developments on the Klein property were

Valley Town Houses (1968) and The Meadows (1985). Colchester Estates West (Cherry Place) was on a good portion of landowner Mankiewicz's eight acres. Previously, it had been farmed by the Parsons, Sprague, Bowers, Fream and Coutean families. Developed by Nathan Korgrok, it was a continuation of nearby Colchester Estates. Prospect Park, built in two sections by Samuel Greenhaus and Sons in 1953, was carved out of land previously farmed by the Abbott, Simmas, James and Meyers families. Though comparatively small, Prospect Park soon established a civic association. One of its leaders, Arthur Leatherman, ran for school board in 1958.

Meadow Brook Farms: Barnum Woods

Barnum's Meadow Brook Farm changed hands and was subdivided a few times. In 1914, Edward Ireland's family remodeled the old mansion. A professional artist and advertising agent who made posters for Metro-Goldwyn-Mayer, Ireland operated St. Kevin's Kennels, breeding famous show dogs (most notably the Irish setter Rory II) and later moving to Meadow Brook Park. Eugene Van Schaick, whose relative Jenkins Van Schaick organized pony races for Hempstead Farm Racing Association in 1891, purchased a five-and-three-fourth-acre tract from Barnum in 1911. Ralph Wattley, president of the National Drug Store Corporation, later resided there and called the estate Glendeavor.

The remainder of the farm was broken up after Maie Barnum married Leo Wanner in 1908. "Meadow Brook Farms" was surveyed for future development in 1911 and sold at auction on November 1. Several key East Meadow roads were mapped at this time: Wilson, Luddington, Durham, Preston and Richmond. On the other side of the brook, streets named Meadow Brook Road and West End Place were created, mostly obliterated by the Meadowbrook Parkway extension in 1954. All the mapped streets north of Wilson (or Christian) Road were strictly theoretical, except part of the Mill Road, which ran from the Barnum estate west to the mill at the brook near 556 Richmond Road.

In 1915, Maie and Leo resided in a new house on the property, now the site of Barnum Woods School playground. Following in her grandmother's footsteps, Maie climbed the social ladder and trained dogs for police and Red Cross work. Her success in obtaining convictions in high-profile cases led to Maie being named the first female deputy police officer in Nassau County in

1 RICHMOND MANOR
2 ROCKVILLE OAKS
3 RICHMOND ESTATES
4 SAMSTEEN ESTATES
5 THERESA ESTATES
6 EAST MEADOW GARDENS
7 PRESTON ESTATES
8 BEL-AIR FARMS
9 MERRICK WOOD HOMES
10 DURHAM HOMES
11 DURHAM ESTATES
12 WINTHROP ESTATES
13 LAKEVILLE ESTATES
14 BLENDWOOD ESTATES
15 BEECHWOOD AT E.M.
16 ROSDEL HOMES

A map of
EAST MEADOW DEVELOPMENTS
in the
BARNUM WOODS AREA
by
SCOTT ECKERS

1917. Her Lewanno Kennels were so popular that famous movie dog Rin Tin Tin was taken there as soon as he was sneaked into America from the battlefields of France. A devastating 1918 fire that destroyed the kennel did not end the operation, which focused on breeding German shepherds. In 1925, following a divorce, Maie sold off more parcels of land and the Barnums' early American furniture. She married for a third time, to cattle rancher Hiram West, and died in Reno, Nevada, in 1931—one week after her mother passed. Arthur Rollin took over the kennel site in 1922 and moved Rollin's Kennels to Hempstead-Bethpage Turnpike in 1926.

In 1928, Silas and Norah Andrews occupied Maie's estate, which they named Sunny Knoll. Silas, a highway contractor, was also president of the Long Island Poultry Association and superintendent of the Mineola Fair. While he raised prize-winning hens, his wife, Norah, focused on running a cattery and serving as president of Cat Fanciers Federation. Their friend and fellow bird enthusiast Edmund Koehler lived on an estate just north called Greengates Farm.

Unlike other East Meadow land surveys of the World War I era (e.g., Hempstead Terrace Gardens), some of the lots in Meadow Brook Farms were developed. Still, a 1938 aerial photograph shows only some homes in the entire development. Additionally, the home sites were much larger: the grid between Merrick Avenue and Preston Road featured two-and-a-half-acre lot sizes. West toward the brook, lot sizes varied between approximately one and two acres, with some larger lots at North Jerusalem Road. Richmond Road curves with the brook, which created some of the smallest building lots; ironically, these are some of the largest in East Meadow today.

In its final days during the 1940s, the "palatial" P.C. Barnum homestead served as Raye and Morton Halsband's Barnum Boarding and Country Day School. The couple owned/directed Camp Lenni-Len-A-Pe upstate and had previously run Mother Goose School/Happy Times Camp out of their Hempstead home. Following an April 1952 fire with three-hundred-foot-high flames that destroyed the vacant Maie Barnum mansion,

Above: Rollin's Kennels, with Maie Barnum mansion in the rear, circa 1923. *Arthur Rollin.*

Right: Maie Barnum Wanner and "Filax," 1919. *American National Red Cross photograph collection, Library of Congress.*

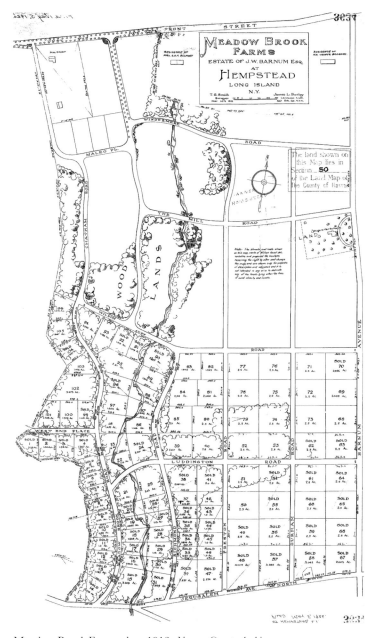

Meadow Brook Farms plan, 1912. *Nassau County Archives.*

Kay Manor.

Irving Kay built the most expensive splits in the area. A large sign at Andrews Lane still welcomes residents to Kay Manor.

Home development companies began buying up the empty Meadow Brook Farms lots and subdividing them into suburban communities around 1950. The first major builder was Herbert Messer and Gino Fubini's Elgin Construction Company. Elgin Homes was developed with Joseph-Martin Homes south of Wilson Road in 1950. A two-bedroom Cape Cod sold for $11,450, and a three-bedroom ranch cost $13,450. Dr. Fubini was previously a civil engineering professor in Torino, Italy. Joseph-Martin Associates (Joseph Shapiro and Martin Buxbaum) built more houses beginning in 1951 and 1952 on land north of Wilson Road, behind today's Apollo Diner. Joseph-Martin advertised its "Del Rio Ranch" quite widely. Models designed by Matern and York on "winding, cul-de-sac safety streets" sold for $10,490, $14,750 and $17,990. Sales agent Ernst Heumann of Trylon Realty became an investor. Shapiro and Buxbaum were highly regarded by the residents of their colonies. In 1954, Joseph-Martin homeowners awarded them a bronze plaque due to their "interest and cooperation in the welfare of our community."

In 1952, "Kal-da" Kalman Klein and David Teicholz expanded their popular Lakeville Estates development. The first section west of Merrick Avenue was built north, east and west of the Barnum Woods School site. Streets in the 1950s were typically named after developers' family members: Kalman's wife was Sylvia, and his first son was Stephan Marc (although the street was actually named after neighborhood designer and associate Stephen Marc). Lakeville Estates Sections 2 and 3 were built in 1953 along Richmond Road. Section 4 was built in the triangle between Bellmore, Merrick and Prospect Avenues, and Section 5 was constructed on one

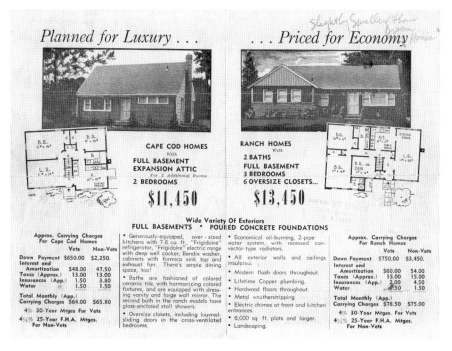

Joseph-Martin Homes brochure. *Bill O'Leary.*

Meadow Brook Farms lot at Luddington Road and Merrick Avenue. A sixth section, not on old Barnum property, was centered on Dieman Lane.

Lots south of Lakeville Estates and Elgin Homes became a true hodgepodge of redevelopment in the mid-1950s. Benjamin Avenue and Blendwood Drive were built as Blendwood Estates by the Stone family in 1950. Louis Entman built Winthrop Estates on Durham Road and Winthrop Drive in 1951. In 1952, Preston Estates rose on Preston Road and Maple Lane. The same year, David Teicholz (of Lakeville Estates) built East Meadow Gardens on Luddington Road, Oak Place, Maple Lane and Preston Road. Kusnitz and Peck developed Durham Homes on Durham Road and Shari Lane in 1953 and Durham Estates Sections 1 and 2 on both sides of Luddington Road in 1955. Bel-Air Farms was a small 1954 development on Luddington Road and Durham Road by Sokolov Brothers and Sons. Between Bel-Air and Durham Homes was a four-home 1955 project by Mark Kane called Merrick Wood Homes.

Rockville Oaks was built on Richmond Road and Richmond Court in 1954 by Mark Kane and Bob and Arthur Pullman. The following year, the same men constructed Richmond Estates at Richmond Road, Sally Court and North Jerusalem Road. Richmond Manor (Bea Court) was developed by Leonard Metz in 1973 behind a convent called International Fraternity of Saint Pius X. The final lots of the old Barnum property were developed on Preston Road as Samstein Estates in 1967 and Theresa Estates in 1983, both on an extension of Sally Court. Finally, Carrie Court was built by Beechwood Estates at East Meadow in 1984.

Until 1862, these lands were part of Moses Smith's farm. The small Smith Family Cemetery was located at 1507 North Jerusalem Road until 1958. The patriarch was Moses's father, Zebulon, whose homestead was the "Sprout Land" on the east side of Merrick Avenue and whose children and grandchildren were related to almost every prominent East Meadow family mentioned in this work: Place, Duryea, Carman, Mollineux, Seaman, Fish and—of course—most of the nineteenth-century Smiths.

Hempstead Farm and Meadowbrook Development Corporation

This section looks at the Prospect Avenue area toward Hempstead Turnpike, on the land that was largely "Hempstead Farm." Hempstead Farm was north of Oscar Lewis Schwencke's Hempstead Lawns Section 4 at Newbridge Avenue, mapped in 1909. Hempstead Lawns Section 3 (Lenox and Noble Streets) and Section 4 (Stuyvesant, Park and Lenox Avenues; Noble Street; and Everett Place) were formerly lands of Anna Willis and family and are now home to some of the oldest homes in East Meadow.

Hempstead Farm was a large property on both sides of Hempstead Turnpike, between Front Street and Newbridge Road. In the nineteenth century, it was used for horse races under leadership of Thomas Terry, the real estate and insurance agent largely responsible for acquisition of lands on which the Brooklyn Bridge was built. Though promoted by leading industrialists of the Gilded Age, the model farm was not a commercial success. In the 1880s, it added a large dog breeding operation with kennels on the northwest corner of Carman Avenue and Hempstead Turnpike. Hempstead Farm concentrated heavily on breeding collies and later expanded to pointers, Great Danes and terriers. J. Pierpont Morgan himself was active; in 1888, he purchased a famous collie named Bendigo from the operation for $1,500 for use at his own, impressive, Kragston Kennels in Highland Falls, New York.

The members of the Meadow Brook Club west of Merrick Avenue, which included many prominent East Meadow residents, would frequently hunt

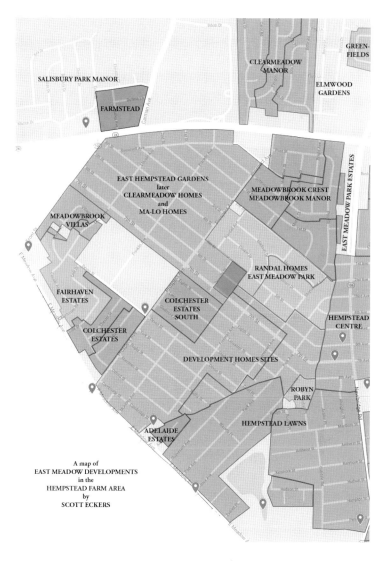

A map of
EAST MEADOW DEVELOPMENTS
in the
HEMPSTEAD FARM AREA
by
SCOTT ECKERS

foxes on the Hempstead Farm property. Hempstead Farm (Horse) Racing Association was an outgrowth of the popularity of the nearby Meadow Brook Club and was promoted by the Queens County Agricultural Society, which felt that it would add to the sport's popularity and help the local economy. Meadow Brook Club members grew to resent the popularity of Hempstead Farm's modern track, which was 480 feet short of a mile and included a grandstand. They felt that Hempstead Farm took away from the prestige of the Meadow Brook Club's races. Still, the growing local popularity of polo among the "society set" contributed to the equestrian industry in East

Meadow at Terry's Hempstead Farm, Joshua Barnum's Meadow Brook Farm and the Salisbury estates. Scores of newspaper articles detail the pony race cups and dog show medals won by Hempstead Farm. Beginning in 1893, Terry ran into financial trouble that caused the corporation to incur significant debt. His stake in the enterprise ended after he was bought out by Morgan.

After the Hempstead Farm's closure, mortgage holders J.P. Morgan, August Belmont, Maurice Holt and Isaac Wolf conveyed more than 410 acres to Wheeler Brothers Agents, which sold the property to William Godnick, Jacob Freedman, Maurice Holt and Isaac Wolff's Meadowbrook Development Corporation. Part of the Hempstead Farm on the north side of Hempstead Turnpike was sold to J.J. Lannin. The former kennel property was subdivided as "Farmstead" in 1933. Within six months, the land south of the turnpike was subdivided. Parcel "A" was sold quickly for hundreds of thousands of dollars. It was generally bound by Roosevelt (formerly Harding) Avenue, Hempstead Turnpike, Front Street, Eighth Street and Prospect Avenue, with a small section between Fifth Street and Eighth Street on the south side of Prospect Avenue.

Parcel "A" became known as East Hempstead Gardens and was developed by brothers John and Frank Roethlein. John, the firm's leader, was past president of the Brooklyn Federation of Catholic Societies and advertised East Hempstead Gardens as a "restricted" community—that is, for sale to Christians only. Roethlein advertised proximity to a new racetrack that was to be built across Hempstead Turnpike (near today's hospital) as well as to the village of Hempstead. In addition to churches, schools and the "best equipped volunteer fire department in the entire state," the company also highlighted the Long Island Motor Parkway and nearby golf courses. Roethlein hired a small army of salesmen, and sales of 1,638 surveyed lots began with an open house on Sunday, June 13, 1926. Like developer O.L. Schwencke, Roethlein Brothers provided free transportation to see the site and stressed the investment value over the homes themselves (which were all brick and sold for $7,750 and up). The firm guaranteed a profit with its "Equity Plan" that would establish a reserve fund from 40 percent of monthly installments and pay landowners should the property be appraised at least 15 percent higher within five years. Roethlein Brothers promised to return 50 percent of payments made if the property did not increase in value.

Although land sales were successful, very few homes were built within the first two decades, and not every planned street was opened. The project

Aerial photograph (1938) of East Hempstead Gardens with few streets opened (*center*), Meadowbrook Hospital (*top*), Newbridge Road School (*extreme bottom right*) and Front Street School (*left*), surrounded by farmland and early developments.

established the grid of numbered streets and laid out the Prospect Avenue extension from its former terminus at Newbridge (now East Meadow) Avenue to Hempstead Turnpike in October 1926. Most of the numbered streets were still unopened by 1947.

Meadowbrook Development Corporation built on a small section of Parcel "A" between Fifth Street and Seventh Street, just south of McKinley Avenue (now DeWolfe Place) in 1929, on which the Gethsemane Church now sits.

Another early housing project resulting from the Meadowbrook Development Corporation purchase was Development Home Sites, built on the south side of Prospect Avenue on two irregularly shaped parcels around McKinley and Freeman Avenues and extensions of Stuyvesant and Park Avenues. The developers did not continue the East Hempstead Gardens numbering system past Eighth Street but maintained the efficient grid pattern so popular before World War II. Construction began in 1932; within six years, there were many more homes built and occupied than in the East Hempstead Gardens section. Curved connections of Fifth through Eighth Streets (today's avenues) of the earlier Hempstead Centre development provided easy access to the newer Newbridge Road School. Housing starts were scarce southwest of Devon Street, and the Oxford and Cambridge Street area was still used for farmland. A small project named Meadowbrook Villas off Front Street at Kodma Place rose in 1940.

Neither East Hempstead Gardens nor Development Home Sites would be completely built up before World War II. Lane Realty sold two-story "East Hempstead Estates" colonial homes for $10,990 in 1948 and 1949. Large numbers of "Queen Ranch Homes" were built in eleven sections over 150 acres by Paul and Nathan Reizen in the area near Devon Street and Prospect Avenue. The Queen Ranch Homes cost $11,990 in 1952 and included attached garages and rear patios. One feature of the model was its ability to support a two-bedroom addition in its "expansion" dormered attic, and many homeowners eventually took advantage of this option. A 1953 development program by Ma-Lo Homes (Anthony Mastroianni and Al Louri) built on empty lots near Third Street and Lincoln Avenue with $13,490 Cape Cod homes.

The baby boom brought rapid development to the Prospect Avenue area, including the former Meadowbrook Development parcels. The largest, Meadowbrook Manor (or Crest), was built by Louis Bright in 1947 and 1948 (hence Bright Avenue) and completed by Joseph-Martin Homes in 1949. Situated just south of Hempstead Turnpike and west of Newbridge Road, he sought to include up to three hundred homes. Buyers were enthusiastic about moving to the suburbs for $8,390, so Bright's ambitious $3 million project rose quicker than expected and was expanded in 1956. Bright constructed the Meadowbrook Shopping Center, where the nascent East Meadow Public Library rented storefronts while the current library was planned and built.

Colchester Estates was built in several sections on both sides of Prospect Avenue in 1950. The initial section, constructed on the former farmlands of Alphonso Fredericks, is centered on Chester and Byrd Drives. Colchester Estates South was built on a parcel of the Meadowbrook Development Corporation at Eighth, Lancaster and Gladmore Streets. Michael Lamm and Saul Seiff of Home Specialists began selling the brick homes in 1949 for $9,350. In 1966, Seiff became the president of the Long Island Builders Institute and was honored by Conservationists United of Long Island for his effort in saving trees in Suffolk County housing projects.

The sizable East Meadow Park (or Randal Homes) development was planned in 1950 by Michel Randal, formerly a Parisian architect, with ranch homes selling for $8,390 and $8,890. Residents of the forty-three-acre development formed a civic association but merged with the East Meadow Taxpayers Association in 1951.

Fairhaven Estates, developed by Myron and Harry Nelkin (his father) and William Krown, followed in 1952. Veterans could purchase in Fairhaven

Library in storefronts of the Meadowbrook Shopping Center. *Howard Kroplick.*

Estates for $11,990, with a down payment of $960. These "Inexpensive Luxury and Priceless Location" homes are situated on the curvy extension of Lincoln Avenue and Cole Drive and, of course, Fairhaven Road. Like other midcentury developments, advertisements stressed the "science" kitchen and ceramic bathroom in addition to a full basement and attached garage, a mainstay of the 1950s. Myron Nelkin rose to prominence in 1983 when he rebuilt the Garden City Hotel. His good fortune led to philanthropy for Jewish causes. Farther down Newbridge Avenue, Harry Ringhoff sold off most of his land in 1957 to create the small Adelaide Estates, named after his wife. Brick-front Cape Cods sold for $16,990 and had customizable second floors.

In 1950, the Town of Hempstead awarded Karlson and Reed a contract for $73,536 to install additional water mains in the central part of East Meadow, largely for the aforementioned housing projects. This was important after a 1948 outbreak of *B. coli* in forty homes was linked to contamination in individual water pumps at Colchester Estates. Without a water district, established in March 1949, the quality of water was hard to regulate. During a transition period in 1950, some East Meadow residents were hooked up

131

to a temporary supply from the well in Salisbury Park, but water pressure was a problem and the newer developments, such as Colchester, were not connected. Notably, the water tower and Meadow Lawn School were built in 1950 on lands ceded for public use at Franklin Avenue and Devon Street. In its early years, the tower was painted a red-and-white checkerboard pattern. Its completion ensured East Meadow a safe water supply for drinking and adequate pressure for fighting fires.

FISH FARM AND WOODLAND AREA

The original planned development in the area bound by Prospect Avenue, Bellmore Avenue, North Jerusalem Road and East Meadow Avenue was Section 3 of Oscar Lewis Schwencke's Hempstead Lawns at Lenox Avenue, Noble Street and Irving Place, carved out of Anna Willis's lands. As was typical with early twentieth-century projects, few lots were developed. Several families constructed homes and used adjacent lots for large lawns or gardens. Beginning in 1953, these empty spaces were built up by August Ihlefeld as Lenox Estates. Homes cost $12,490 and featured knotty pine cabinets and super-modern Formica work surfaces. Like other developments in the neighborhood, the Cape Cod houses were designed by Alwin Cassens Jr., well-known architect of small single-family homes. He was the author of *Ranch Homes for Today* (1953), which has been regarded as a significant contribution to American Midcentury Modern design. Stock plans for the homes—complete with period-appropriate descriptions like "Honey of a Rambler," "When You Settle Down," "Ranch House Step-Saver," "Overall Comfort," "Meet Today's High Standards," "With a Homey Effect" and "Shipshape and Expandable"—could be purchased by developers. Cassens is the namesake of the Carnegie Mellon University Memorial Fund in Architecture.

The largest early development on the west side of Newbridge Avenue was East Hempstead Park by Powers East Hempstead Inc. As the name suggests, this was the large farm of John Powers and family (who formerly had properties along Newbridge Road). After it was sold and subdivided in 1928, a numbered street system was established (First through Ninth Streets, perpendicular with Powers Avenue). Due to confusion with the numbered grid growing a few blocks northeast, East Hempstead Park streets adopted new names in 1933, but most were paths to nowhere. Almost every home in this development was built in 1949.

A map of
EAST MEADOW DEVELOPMENTS
in the
WOODLAND AREA
by
SCOTT ECKERS

A significant builder in East Meadow was Central Developing Corporation, which previously built up much of Valley Stream. The name Central Homes is derived from Central Avenue in that village. In East Meadow, David Weisbarth and his son-in-law, Irving Newman, bought large tracts of land from long-established farming families (e.g., Fish) and quickly transformed the orchards and fields into suburban sprawl. Sections 1–3 were the original 1950 and 1951 Central Manor homes designed by Alwin Cassens Jr. The $11,790 Beaumont model featured automatic kitchen equipment; the smaller $10,690 Arkansas model featured an expansion attic. Unlike Levitt houses built at the same time, Central Homes incorporated basements. Model houses were built at North Jerusalem Road and Wilson Avenue. Like other early 1950s developments in East Meadow, Central Homes highlighted G.I. Bill benefits: veterans could buy the homes with no down payment. Weisbarth and Newman built Central Manor Stores adjacent to the homes, and Nassau County built "New" North Jerusalem Road between the homes and the stores to straighten the road. (Ennabrock Road is the original North

Central Homes.

Jerusalem Road segment.) The county also built a larger-than-typical storm basin north of the new road, at the location of a former pond on the Raymond Fish farm.

Central Homes Section 4, built in 1951, and Section 5, built in 1953, were larger $16,500 split-level homes (Cynthia Drive, Andrea Road and Chaladay and Harvey Lanes). The northern part of the property, lands formerly of Samuel Seabury, was undeveloped as originally planned and sold to the East Meadow UFSD for the erection of the future Woodland Junior High School. Section 6 was built across North Jerusalem Road, on an extension of Jackson Place in North Bellmore in 1954. These brick and stone homes were sold with the most modern Hotpoint kitchen appliances, a direct appeal to postwar women. Section 7, at Bellmore Avenue and Newman Road behind the old Seaman homestead, was marketed as Midlawn Development by David Weisbarth and Irving, Al and Louis Newman in 1956 and 1957. Midlawn featured brick split-level houses costing $21,990 and $23,990, which was quite expensive for the time. Part of this tract (just south of Newman Road) was the small estate of farmer George Littleton and his wife, Sarah. Their home, Evergreen Cottage, was purchased from Prudence Baldwin in 1905 and frequented by guests—friends and relatives from their former home on East Thirty-Fourth Street in New York City—seeking the clean country air. Aside from taking boarders, "Farmer Littleton" and his wife kept pets, raised pigeons and grew grapes. Sarah kept a homer pigeon for almost twenty years—an impressive lifespan indeed. Two modern poultry houses were added in 1907. By 1909, both George and Sarah were suffering health problems that required frequent medical care, affecting productivity.

The builders of Central Homes expanded their empire even further in 1956 and 1957 when Irving Newman, Hy Berchansky and Stanley Grogstein constructed $19,990 homes in Cynron Estates at Cynron and Karen Lanes. Under Noble Homes Inc., David's father, Jacob Weisbarth, built Midland Gardens in the Midland Drive and Meadow Lane area in 1953. Like Central Homes, the $11,750 and $12,990 models had washing machines and expansion attics. Veterans could purchase homes with favorable terms, such as a 5 percent down payment. Midland Gardens had been the former Frawlick property and the home of the Melvin family in the nineteenth century.

The vast majority of homes built in East Meadow in the 1950s were planned and constructed by Jews. For families moving to East Meadow from Brooklyn and Queens, the existence of a Conservative synagogue within walking distance was a major draw. Therefore, several developers of the baby boom era made sure to provide such a service for their current—and prospective—customers. Jacob's son George (David's brother) founded East Meadow Jewish Center in July 1953. As a result, several neighborhoods in East Meadow became predominantly Jewish.

Jewish Center members initially met in their homes, the Republican Club and storefronts. The congregation dedicated its first building during Chanukah in 1956. Located upstairs was a combination sanctuary/

EAST MEADOW JEWISH CENTER

KISLEV, 5717
Vol. IV, No. 3   NOVEMBER, 1956

CHANUKAH ✡ ☸ ☸ DEDICATION
NOVEMBER 29th — DECEMBER 6th

By a happy coincidence, Chanukah this year offers us cause for a triple celebration.

First, we commemorate, as we do each Chanukah, the rededication of the Temple in 167 B.C.E. when the Maccabees were victorious in their struggle against the Syrians.

Second, we chose to schedule the dedication of our own Center building with the Chanukah festival.

Third, November 29th, the first day of Chanukah this year, marks the 9th anniversary of the United Nations' decision to partition Palestine, and so set up the State of Israel, a step that brought joy to Jews all over the world and realization to those who had been personally fighting to bring the State of Israel into existence.

East Meadow Jewish Center.

auditorium and downstairs a religious school wing. Growth was so rapid that by 1963, the congregation had broken ground on a large new sanctuary that increased capacity to 1,800 worshippers. Trustee Joseph Rothstein was a major force behind the synagogue's success. Major expansions increased the footprint in 1964 and 1987. At the height of the baby boom, more than nine hundred member families, mostly from Prospect Avenue and Barnum Woods, sent their children to Hebrew school at East Meadow Jewish Center. Rabbi Israel Nobel and Cantor Paul Carus served the congregation into the 1980s; Rabbi Dr. Ronald Androphy has been the spiritual leader since 1983. In 2020, Temple Beth El of Bellmore joined with EMJC.

For Jews interested in Yiddish and social justice, the Nassau Cultural Center of the Arbeter Ring/Workmen's Circle operated on East Meadow Avenue from 1954 to 2022. This unimposing and unique branch housed the I.L. Peretz folk "shule" for children, led principally by Mikhl Baran and his daughter Ruth. It is the oldest Jewish secular school in Nassau County to be chartered by the State Board of Regents.

The lands on which Central Homes (sections 1–5) and Wenwood Oaks developments were built was the sizable Fish property, which famously consisted of peach orchards (growing from one hundred trees in 1898 to one thousand trees by World War II). Samuel Fish purchased the land from Jeremiah Robbins and established his farm there in 1838. The house at the corner of North Jerusalem Road and Newbridge Avenue was used for six generations, although it was remodeled in 1901 and moved to another part of the property in 1926. Throughout the years, the farm evolved and modernized but never lost the country charm of years past. Each September, peaches were king, but the family also grew wheat and flax plus Long Island staples potatoes and corn. The Fish family's farm became so notable that it was highlighted in the 1947 publication *Century Farms of New York State*.

Samuel Doty Fish (1832–1884) and his wife, Elizabeth Emily (1838–1912), lived on the one-hundred-acre North Jerusalem Road property prior to the Civil War. Fish was involved with the Queens County Game Protective Association, run by Joshua Barnum. The Protective Association was formed in 1887 with the purpose of "enforcing the game laws of the State, to preserve land, and to stock the preserves with birds." In 1889, the organization populated East Meadow area with quail brought from Tennessee. Samuel Doty Fish appears to be the descendant of Samuel Doty (1743–1823) and Catherine Baldwin (1745–1823), who moved to the area during the American Revolution. Doty's ancestry, and that of the Sprague

Fish Homestead. *Hoeffner family.*

family with whom they married, can be traced all the way to the *Mayflower* and Plymouth Plantation.

Samuel and Elizabeth Fish's son George (1859–1946) and his wife, Martha (1860–1953), raised several children on the farm after the Civil War. They held fairs and lively suppers on their farm to benefit the Methodist Episcopal Church. At the turn of the century, George served as president of the board of trustees for East Meadow Hall. One of their sons, Raymond George Fish (1888–1970), married Mary Williams (1885–1958) and brought up his children on the same property. Both he and his son, Raymond George Fish Jr., served in leadership positions in civic, church and school matters, with the elder Raymond serving for a time as board of education president. Like many of their neighbors, the Fishes became truck farmers.

Amelia Fish (1803–1989) lived on Hempstead-Bethpage Turnpike (at the site of Nassau University Medical Center) with William and John, her children, and their families. William's son Elbert Buchanan Fish (1840–1927), who oversaw local roads, owned the property until it was sold and incorporated into the Hempstead Farm. In 1867, Elbert escaped certain injury when his horse was startled by a train at the Hempstead LIRR station.

Elbert was dragged half a mile before his carriage smashed into another vehicle filled with bricks. He landed under the broken wagon, was dragged even farther and—somewhat miraculously—eventually stopped his horse. The Fishes of Hempstead Turnpike were likely cousins of the Fishes of North Jerusalem Road and of their neighbors, the Doty family.

Sidney Weniger of Greenwood Construction Corporation built Wenwood Oaks around Wenwood and Bruce Drives on land sold by June Sokolov. Sidney's father, Morris, started Wenwood Organization, a home building business in New York City. Morris Weniger and Sons Inc. created developments all over Long Island. Sidney's son Bruce (the street's namesake) recalled, "Almost all the projects started with 'Wen,' including 'Wenshaw Park' ('Shaw' was a derivative of Moe Shore's family name, my uncle in [the] North Merrick project), Wenwood at Bar Harbour (Massapequa Park, where there is another Wenwood Drive, among others in East Meadow, Brookville, North Bellmore and Hauppauge), Wenwood at Selden, etc." Sidney Weniger later expanded his real estate dealings under Wengroup Companies and focused heavily on emerging markets in New York, and later Arkansas, becoming known for extravagant parties before going out of business in 1990. In East Meadow, three models were available: the $15,950 Barden split, the $17,750 Wenwood split and the $18,250 brick Glencote ranch. Advertisements featured a "finished knotty pine rumpus and recreation room." Ken Zuckerman, an original resident, recalled a story of how a mosquito fog truck would come through Wenwood Oaks with all the children happily running behind! Wenwood Oaks still has an active civic association.

Sy Nemirov and David Tuchman of Meryl Estates Inc. constructed several small sections of houses around Central Homes in 1953. Known as Meryl Manor and Landers Park, these are primarily on Bethlynn Court and Leslie Lane. Patsy Esposito built and sold four houses on her land (Esposito Court) in 1957. Four houses on the adjacent property were constructed much later. The Kirsch Fur Farm operated on Chaladay Lane. Emanuel Rosenberg and Stanley and Marvin Gerla of Gerose Estates built the small San Remo Rancher Colony on Chaladay Lane and Gerose Estates on Gerose Court in 1952. Houses were made of brick and cedar and sold for $15,990. Their San Remo Rancher model was advertised with a "Beautiful Hollywood Kitchen." Part of the land for these developments had been in the L'Ambrose family, whose pre-development home still stands on North Jerusalem Road. Historically, the intersection, including a small grassy piece that is now between the old and new road alignments, had been settled by the Seaman family, although

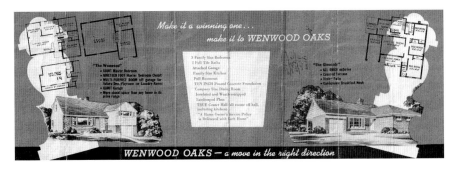

Wenwood Oaks. *David Meyer.*

Kate Vail Barnum came to own the tract in the early twentieth century. Just across North Jerusalem Road, Rosenberg and Gerla also built Cameo at East Meadow, which is technically in North Bellmore. There is an old private cemetery just across from Cameo Estates at Bradley Court.

Lakeville Estates Section 6 was built by Kalman Klein and David Teicholz on Dieman, Garden, Flower and Pine Lanes—an irregularly shaped collection of properties—in 1954. The same year, Sy Corak and Michael Chaiko (Syntal Realty Company and Cor-Mar Realty Corporation) built the widely advertised Broadlawn Estates. This development—built in three parallel sections as Mark Drive, Reed Drive, Sherwood Drive and Sylvan Lane—was alternatively known as Sherwood Park. Homes were designed as front-to-back and "Holiday" splits and were initially sold for $19,990 to $23,000. Residents formed the Broadlawn Civic Association. An extension of Maxwell Drive was built on the fur farm lands as Maxwell Estates in 1961 by the Chaladay Lane Development Corporation. A section of Broadlawn Estates had been the Nohern (or Nohearn) family farm. Family patriarch Nathan Nohern was a celebrated and active member of the Methodist Episcopal Church, having held many leadership positions there. His son Irving and Isabelle Fream's old home still exists on Bellmore Avenue. They grew sugar corn and other vegetables there for sale to the New York City market. The Fream family lived southwest of the East Meadow Hotel, on what is today the pool parking lot, and north at the corner of Prospect and Newbridge Avenues.

Billed as the "last land in East Meadow," Jack Weiner's East Meadow Estates Inc. constructed Tall Oaks on the last remaining section of the former Raymond Fish homestead between 1959 and 1961. These houses on Clover Court, with a very early '60s feel, were built on the south edge of apple orchards, just across the street from Oberle's Florist.

Several smaller homesteads along the main roads were sold off for development as the large tracts around them fell to suburban sprawl. Vincent Berger, who later built on the Klein property at Front Street, created Avington Homes in 1951. These twenty-two homes at Von Elm Avenue were designed by popular architect Stanley Klein and included large picture windows, wrought-iron railings, knotty pine cabinets, Formica tops and Venetian blinds. Great Oaks Development Corporation built Barbara Park in 1957, where photographer/historian Steve Buczak (or Boschock) spent his childhood. The following year brought Prospect Estates, eight homes on an extension of Chamberlain Street. This section of Prospect Avenue was historically settled by the Valentine, Smith, Seaman, Post and Fream families. The Post, Fream and Nohern families became related through marriage.

Aerial photo of southern East Meadow in 1954, showing new developments off Prospect Avenue, Bellmore Avenue and North Jerusalem Road. *Author's collection.*

Lemax Homes developed a tract of land abutting Central Homes in 1962. This small neighborhood is unique because it is in East Meadow but served by the North Bellmore Post Office. This inconsistency is due to the county's 1950 realignment of North Jerusalem Road.

The superblock also includes some of East Meadow's newest housing developments. A formerly undeveloped piece of the Fish farm was built up by Donald Voorhis's Fams Homes in 1971. After the East Meadow UFSD sold the Prospect Avenue School property to Living House Inc., Heritage Park was created on extensions on Benito, Adelphi and Coakley Streets in 1979. Finally, the year 1986 brought MED Associates' Greenhouse Homes on Poe Avenue. This lot was formerly used for Goldblatt's sand pit operations.

Between Merrick and Bellmore Avenues

The triangular neighborhood west of Bellmore Avenue, east of Merrick Avenue and north of North Jerusalem Road consists of three developments. The earliest (and largest), centered on Stratford Drive, was planned between 1947 and 1949 by Louis Sokolov Brothers and Sons. Marlen Homes, as it was known, was built on property that had been farmed for generations. In the nineteenth century, Jotham Post and Benjamin Post lived there; in 1859, the land was owned by Elbert Smith. At some time before 1873, it was purchased by P.C. Barnum. His daughter Kate Vail Barnum inherited this part of her parents' estate in 1893. By 1914, she had sold off that part of the property to the family of Leo Levy, who still owned it in 1927. Prior to World War II, the Stoller family owned it. A small parcel at the southeast corner of Merrick and Prospect Avenues was rezoned to business in 1949, following purchase by the Sokolovs. Three prewar homes from the old families remain on Bellmore Avenue.

Model homes were marketed toward veterans and nonveterans in 1948 and 1949. By 1950, 123 out of 153 planned dwellings in Marlen Homes were sold. The Cape Cods featured sliding-door closets and were priced at an affordable $9,500 and $9,990. Their apparent popularity brought the price up by $1,000 later that year. In 1950 and 1951, small ranch houses designed by Karl Block went on sale for $12,990. They included tiled bathrooms, expansion attics, patios and attached garages, of course—all essential features of the quintessential East Meadow early 1950s home.

In 1956, the Sokolovs were involved with the Sadkins, Wenigers and other local developers in the creation and operation of a corporate suburban real estate syndicate called All-State Properties. Howard Teas and Ernest Steinbrenner of Teas and Steinbrenner, one of the most important survey companies of the period, joined the group to venture into real estate development. Teas was president of Nassau Suffolk Civil Engineers in 1953. Working together, All-State built a considerable percentage of Long Island homes in the 1950s. For instance, Morris Sokolov and Herbert Sadkin worked together building many "Birchwood" developments under various corporate entities.

Just east of Marlen Homes rose Paul-Lee Homes, led by H. Rosen and Son (Hyman and Leo Rosen). Paul-Lee Homes, likely named for Pauline and Leo Rosen, was built on the Stringham property. The Stringhams had owned this tract of land for many generations—one of the longest continually held properties in East Meadow. Benjamin Stringham seems to have come to East Meadow through his employment as a laborer on P.C. Barnum's farm around 1850, although his ancestors (originally de Tringham) had been in the town of Hempstead since the seventeenth century and were distantly related through marriage to the Carmans and Browers, other early East Meadow families. By 1857, Benjamin had obtained a mortgage on some of the Barnum property on Bellmore Avenue and was living there with Mary Riley, his wife of two years. Their six children were raised in East Meadow; the property was taken over by their son Elmer, who in turn married Hariett "Hattie" Cloudman and raised their own seven children on the farm until moving away in 1914.

When driving or walking through the neighborhood, notice the distinctive cul-de-sac-esque arrangements in the middle of Barbara, Paula and Carla Lanes. The streets were established by Marlen Homes and originally ended

Elmer and Hattie Stringham.

at the cul-de-sacs but were extended toward Bellmore Avenue when Paul-Lee Homes was planned in 1950. Rosen offered his three-bedroom Paul-Lee Homes, laid out in the typical style with basements and attached garages, for $13,490. The two-bedroom model was $1,000 cheaper.

Little Whaleneck Road, which previously ended at North Jerusalem Road, was extended into the neighborhood in 1953 for the creation of Rocco Homes. The community of brick split-level homes was completed in 1955. This section belonged to James Seaman, a wheelwright, in the nineteenth century. Around the turn of the twentieth century, the land belonged to Amos and Carrie Rhodes. Prior to suburban development, the property was Steven and Annie Olish's vegetable farm. The Olishes, originally from Poland, raised their twelve children there. Their neighbors were Willet and Elsebert (William and Elizabeth) Vandewater. Curiously, the 1920 census enumerator (and neighbor) John Seaman referred to North Jerusalem Road as Seaman Avenue. There is no indication that the road was even known as such outside his opportunistic census records. Another unusual substitution found on his records was "Fisher's Avenue" for Prospect Avenue.

SABIA'S CORNER AND NEWBRIDGE ROAD

Pasquale "Patsy" Sabia arrived as an Italian immigrant in 1889 and married Maria "Mary" Rizzo in Brooklyn in 1897. By 1915, the couple had moved to North Bellmore and raised most of their children there. In the 1920s, they settled in the triangle of land bound by North Jerusalem Road, Newbridge Road and Newbridge Avenue, subdivided in 1910 by O.L. Schwencke Land and Investment Company's Hempstead Lawns development (Section 6). Patsy established a general store on lot number one at the southwest corner, which was originally set aside by Schwencke as a hotel site. The Sabias had five sons and five daughters, many of whom lived at or near the same intersection after growing up and starting their own families. The main building of today's Big Chief Day Camp was the home of Patsy's son John and his family. Since 1954, Big Chief has been a fixture in the neighborhood, run by the Picinich family.

Sabia relatives lived on Sherman Avenue, just east of the corner in another Schwencke development called Bellmore Park (Section 1). The family was so large and so prominent in this "Little Italy" section of East Meadow and North Bellmore that the intersection of North Jerusalem and Newbridge Roads became known as Sabia's Corner. Fred, the youngest child, died

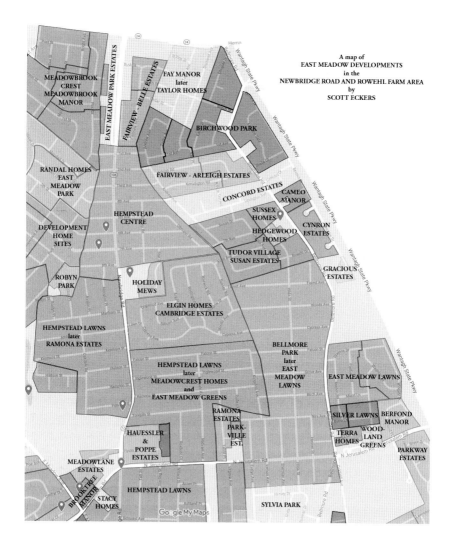

A map of
EAST MEADOW DEVELOPMENTS
in the
NEWBRIDGE ROAD AND ROWEHL FARM AREA
by
SCOTT ECKERS

in 2010. He still lived in the family home at 2424 North Jerusalem Road, constructed circa 1920. This home and the one directly behind it at 704 Newbridge Road, which once served as Patsy's store, survive as private residences today. Until 1951, a chicken house and greenhouse were located between them.

Several families settled on the northeast corner, the longest being the Browers throughout much of the nineteenth century. Lewis Brower, who acquired additional land from Charles Cornelius in 1854, was infamous in East Meadow for attempting to murder his wife in 1887. The Browers also lived on the property that became Oberle's. Just east of the Browers, on both sides of North Jerusalem Road, lived James and Henry Fenn's family. Both sides became part of the Hempstead Lawns development in 1910. Life in this section of East Meadow was quite agrarian in nature. Bernard and George Powers, dairy farmers of Newbridge Road just north of the corner, were insulted when the *Brooklyn Times Union* published an accusation that their cows were afflicted with pleuropneumonia. Their former neighbor, Carman Cornelius, helped quiet the business-ending rumor.

In the late nineteenth century, George Augustus Mott (1835–1906) held property on both sides of North Jerusalem Road. Mott was a prominent lawyer who descended from original English settlers, some of whom were town of Hempstead pioneers. Born in Lynbrook, Mott joined the bar in 1863 and spent decades as a criminal defense attorney. He edited the *Nassau Recorder* and the *Queens County Advance*. The homestead he established at the future Sabia's Corner was payment for legal services rendered to Lewis Brower. Mott was married three times (once, as it was later revealed, to Harriet Gumbs Black, who had not been divorced from her previous husband, Samuel Crawford). Mott fathered fifteen children, but his marital troubles caused estrangement from some of them—especially John Adrian George Mott, who wrote a scathing letter to his father in 1899 calling his new (and very young) wife, Emma Harriet Engels, a gold digger and chastising him for the way he treated the deceased Harriet and their children. Mott bequeathed his property to all his children except John. In a lengthy probate court fight, it came to light that Emma destroyed deeds and wills that left the East Meadow farm and homestead to George's children from Harriet.

Emil Oberle came to East Meadow in 1924 and erected greenhouses on eight acres of land at the corner of Newbridge Avenue and North Jerusalem Road that had previously been part of the Mott estate. Joan Swedberg's family arrived in East Meadow from Phoenix in 1936 and settled on Stuyvesant Avenue. The two were grade school sweethearts at Newbridge Road School. After the eighth grade, the students boarded a "dilapidated bus" from Sabia's Corner to Hempstead High School and married soon after graduating. According to Joan, that section of the hamlet was "a few houses but primarily woods" but "a nice place to grow up." Residents received mail through Hicksville's rural delivery.

Families walked through the old graveyard to get to Sunday school at the Methodist church, and teenagers would hang out at Pollack's candy store near Kenmore Street. Mr. Fish, who owned a peach orchard and farm across the street, would show Emil different farming technology, even though the locals plowed with horses. The Oberles operated the greenhouses and florist

Oberle's Florist. *Oberle.*

shop for three generations, slowly selling off sections of former farmland to developers. In 1981, the Newbridge Development Corporation purchased the land abutting North Jerusalem Road to build Brooktree Manor homes after a 1974 shopping center plan faced local opposition. The florist operated until selling the land in 2016 for condominium development.

As the years passed, the northeast corner was owned by Fred Graebel, Peter Peterson, William Hauessler Jr. and then Charles and Emily Poppe. The sale of their lands first created Poppy and then Hauessler (now Hysler) Streets, parts of which were developed by the James F. Michel Realty Corporation, Ernest Hackwith, Cestare Steel Frame Houses and Saxon Manor Estates. Further development was completed by the Hedgewood Construction Company in 1956 and 1959.

The Poppes' lot on the west side of Newbridge Road was just south of that of Ignatius Bildzukewicz, which became Meadowlane Estates in 1982. Next to Bildzukewicz was Herbert Goldblatt, owner of the well-known sand pit. Most of the land on both sides of Newbridge Road around these properties was developed by Oscar Lewis Schwencke. Hempstead Lawns Section 10, generally west of Newbridge Road and centered on Oakdale Road, was built beginning in 1922. Additional homes were built in 1952–53 as Harry Stern and David Forman's Ramona Estates and Frank and Sid Farber's Budget-Built Bungalows. Section 9, east of Newbridge Road and generally south of Falcon Street and west of Kingston Avenue, was built on the Powers (later Swan) farm beginning in 1922. In the 1950s, it was further developed as Meadowcrest Homes and by Sol Kaplan, Louis Heller and Joseph Schneider as East Meadow Greens at Ramona Street ($11,990 Cassens "New Englander" Cape Cods featuring, of course, knotty pine kitchens, full basements and expansion attics).

The large area east of Section 9 was also planned by Schwencke as Section 1 of his Bellmore Park developments. The land west of Bellmore Road was part of the large Rowehl and Granz nursery farm and Kate Vail Barnum's holdings and was sold off beginning in 1909. It included a small section of North Bellmore. Undeveloped lots were later built up in 1953 by Louis Heller and Joseph Schneider. Just west was Section 8, built along Virginia Avenue in North Bellmore in 1921. Across the street in East Meadow was Ramona Estates (1954) and Parkville Estates (Mike Silveri and Sons, 1959), constructed on the Splitdorf property.

Hempstead Centre was planned on numbered avenues on both sides of Newbridge Road by Rabington in 1926. Similar to Hempstead Lawns, some lots saw quick construction, but most sat vacant until after World War II. John Roreck built Hempstead Centre Homes in 1949–50. The "delightful fieldstone and asbestos shingle homes" with attached garages, sundecks and room for expansion sold for $10,000 (only $500 down for GIs). Nassau County Nursery occupied lots at Seventh Street, west of Newbridge Road.

Jack Weiner and William Marberg ("Marjack Realty") sold land abutting Newbridge Road School to Herbert Messer and Gino Fubini, who built Elgin Homes' Cambridge Estates in 1949. This early suburban subdivision at Lawn Drive, with $8,990 brick and masonry ranches, was abuzz in 1950 due to faulty heating. The Federal Housing Administration stepped in and forced Elgin's president, Fubini, to make repairs to metal ducts that were supposed to have been encased in cement. When the proposed fix was deemed inadequate and residents were claiming it took eleven gallons of oil to heat their homes each day, James Farmer called on the Elgin Estates Home Owners' Association to picket the model home, which fifty people did from April to June, until an injunction prevented them from demonstrating indefinitely. Faced with similar heating woes, Joseph-Martin homeowners from Louis Bright's Meadowbrook Crest worked together to demand FHA/VA intervention, since most were veterans purchasing homes under the G.I. Bill. (Messer and Bright had collaborated). Further misfortune came in June 1952 when an enormous flood affected thirty homes. The Red Cross had to evacuate residents and set them up in a temporary shelter at Temple Emanu-El. Homeowners blamed the county for inadequate sump capacity. Sewers were not yet installed. After Newbridge Road School closed, Holiday Mews was built on its former ballfields in 1981.

David, George and Edward Strausman's "Belle Estates" of their "Fairview Country Home Communities" was constructed along Fairview Avenue in 1950. This development at Newbridge Road and Hempstead Turnpike was Strausman Construction Company's first medium-priced venture. "California-style" homes designed by Rudolph Matern and Herman York selling for $9,290 (no down payment for veterans) featured Kelvinator appliances and '50s touches such as "glamorous bath vanity with Formica top." They would go on to build Arleigh and Salisbury Estates under the Fairview brand. Across Newbridge Road, Herman Lazarus offered homes in his East Meadow Park Estates in 1955 for $16,990.

The easternmost section of East Meadow—between Bellmore Road and the Wantagh Parkway—was built on land once known as Dun Ponds and the Albertson Farm, then part of the Jerusalem School District. In March 1904, Desmond Dunne and Mirabeau Towns purchased 567 acres of old farmland from Isaac Clothier for $45,000. It was further subdivided and settled by farmers of Italian ancestry. In 1953, Louis Heller and Joseph Schneider partnered with Herbert and Seymour Sadkin and Morris Schoenfeld to build the "sought-after, fashionable, investment-wise" East

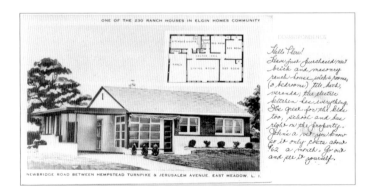

Elgin Homes postcard.

East Meadow Lawns.

Meadow Lawns "Beljer Park" community there, close to their East Meadow Greens project. Two models, the $15,290 Superior Split and $14,590 Royal Ranch, were available in "a community boasting fine homes and flowering gardens and tree-shaded lawns." A sign of the times, buyers chose the split for almost every lot. They were nearly identical to those in Wenwood Oaks.

Lawns Civic Association, formed soon after, held social gatherings and partnered with nearby associations to keep teenagers engaged. Mike Silveri built Silver Lawns, a community of split-level homes, in 1955. The same year, Abraham Berfond and Julius Miller developed Berfond Manor (North Meadow Estates). Civic associations from these three developments came together with the Parkway School PTA in 1957 to oppose a proposed Nike missile repair facility across North Jerusalem Road, at the site of the Mitchel Field radio range transmitter. The same year, John Maraffi built Woodland Greens. Terra Homes was built on most of the Orso farm in 1965.

A German Farming Neighborhood

German-influenced street names (Rowehl, Hilda, Granz and so on) off Bellmore Road are the result of land sales from a prominent farming family on East Meadow's eastern edge. The Rowehl family owned 219 acres south of Hempstead Turnpike and, for four generations, became a significant part of the local economy and culture. In 1854, Diedrich Gerhard Rowehl purchased the land from Theodore and Pauline Pietycker. Their task was to clear the thick brush that covered the entire Hempstead, or "Brushy," Plains area and make the land suitable for farming. The original homestead was constructed—and still stands—at 177 Bellmore Road.

Potatoes were king on the fields—the healthy crop was cultivated and used locally. The Rowehls subsisted on selling potatoes and hay to places like Cooper's Field in Hempstead. Forty-eight descendants of the original settler made their homes on the property and worked in the family's farming business. The Rowehl and Granz families became notable for a large nursery that included greenhouses, barns and a windmill for power. They were "truck farmers" and made their living off the ever-growing New York City population's need for food. Vegetables they grew were taken by horse, and later by motor vehicle, to Wallabout Market in Brooklyn for sale. A simple trip to the Brooklyn marketplace could take nine hours.

By the 1890s, business was booming. The *Queens County Sentinel* reported in 1897 that "Messrs. Rowehl & Granz, the enterprising nurserymen, are doing a rushing business in shrubs and fruit trees." The writers urged "lovers of the beautiful" to visit the family's nurseries. The following year, the paper reported that they "are busily engaged in placing trees and plants around the premises of O.H.P. Belmont." Belmont's mansion on Front Street was no small matter!

The Rowehl property was on a southern extension of Old Westbury Road, which today is largely truncated and forms the northernmost section of Bellmore Road. Bellmore Road itself does not appear on any local maps north of North Jerusalem Road until 1906 but was likely built by the turn of the century, as the original 219-acre homestead was divided into three lots and then again into six sections. Remarkably, all nine properties from the nineteenth and early twentieth centuries survive to this day. One of these, the family's retirement home, was moved east when the Wantagh Parkway was built through the estate. Today, it is Dalton Funeral Home. Another, home to Charles Rowehl and located at 294 Bellmore Road, was purchased by the American Legion's Christian Wolf Post No. 1082. John, Sis and

Rowehl Homestead at 176 Bellmore Road. *Reimels.*

Buster Reimels lived at 176 Bellmore Road. During the Great Depression of the 1930s, the family still had an outhouse. The remaining structures can easily be seen from the road.

A section was sold to Albert Berg, who farmed on the turnpike's north side. Berg's property south of the turnpike was surveyed as Fay Manor in 1925 and sat mostly vacant until Abraham Okun and Joseph Turitz developed Taylor Homes in 1951. Veterans could buy a home featuring "beautiful Hollywood ceramic tile baths" and "'Futuristic' science kitchens" with only $825 down. 1950s development was swift. From north to south, they were the following:

Well-known team Morris Sosnow and Leonard "Len" Schwartz (Morlen Homes) built Birchwood Park Homes from 1950 to 1953. Taylor and Diamond Avenues continue the adjacent Fay Manor map; those streets in Section 5 across Bellmore Road are named for his children Bernice, Lorraine and Sheila. Four $12,990 to $13,490 Stanley Klein–designed models included his typical expansion features and "science" kitchen.

David Strausman worked with architect Rudolph Matern to create a very '50s feel in his Fairview section called Arleigh Estates in 1950. Three-bedroom ranch homes with "pass-thru" bars in the kitchens were sold for $10,290.

Concord Estates, 1960.

"Escape from the city...into a new, carefree life!" boasted Nelkin & Lucente of Concord Estates in 1950. The $10,250 base homes prominently featured refrigerators, washing machines, electric ranges, full basements and expansion attics with rough plumbing already installed. Like neighboring developments, veterans could buy homes through the G.I. Bill, and civilians could obtain loans through the FHA. Ten years later, advertisements said that the small development "Captures the Ageless Charm of Colonial Americana" and stressed the school district's "full sessions!" The $22,490 homes were highly customizable.

Susan Estates was built in 1951–52 as part of the Sadkin-Sadkin-Schoenfeld "Tudor Village" project of $10,990 ranch-colonial homes. Like their other projects, Klein-designed houses had baths in varied colors and fully automatic kitchens and were built to accommodate future second floors (which most homes now have). Veterans could use the builders' own installment plan: $300 down and $15 per week. Across Bellmore Road, Irving Newman, Hy Berchansky and Stanley Grogstein built Cynron Estates, $14,990 homes designed by Alwin Cassens Jr. Just south sits Gracious Estates (1966). The final Rowehl lands became Weissbluth's 1959 Sussex Homes, Hedgewood Homes (1961) and Cameo Manor (1974).

LEVITT HOMES: BUILT ON RESTRICTION AND CORRUPTION

THE TENANT AGREES NOT TO PERMIT THE PREMISES TO BE USED OR OCCUPIED BY ANY PERSON OTHER THAN MEMBERS OF THE CAUCASIAN RACE BUT THE EMPLOYMENT AND MAINTENANCE OF OTHER THAN CAUCASIAN DOMESTIC SERVANTS SHALL BE PERMITTED.
—Levittown Corporation lease, 1948

This clause, number twenty-five on the official lease that tenants signed with the option to buy, has been the subject of debate, strife, lawsuits, regulations, court cases and historians for decades. If you own a Levitt house, see if your deed has this restrictive covenant. It's directly under another bolded clause, number twenty-four, directing you to "cut or cause to be cut the lawn and remove or cause to be removed tall growing weeds at least once a week." It was apparently acceptable to hire a Black gardener.

Levittown—the development, before it was a separate post office or school district—was started in 1947 and was the first and best-known major planned suburban development in America. Six thousand homes were planned on about one thousand acres of former potato fields in Island Trees, just east of East Meadow. William Levitt's project extended beyond what is known as "Levittown" today and ultimately included about seventeen thousand homes.

William "Bill" Levitt and his family were directly involved in the planning of the community, but it was not their first. Earlier developments on the East Coast allowed the brothers to work out an assembly line type of construction inspired by carmaker Henry Ford. Alfred Levitt designed a twenty-seven-step, mass-production construction technique that enabled the company to build 180 homes per week. His father, Abraham, directed the careful landscaping of the lawns, with two trees per home. Brother Bill was heavily involved in the company's marketing strategy, appearing in advertisements, giving interviews for articles and posing for publicity photographs.

Levitt and Sons employed vertical integration techniques to bring down the price of the company's homes. They bought up forests for lumber, manufactured their own nails and repurposed old LIRR tracks, orchestrating exact deliveries by train and truck. Notably, Levitt managed to change zoning laws to exclude basements, despite significant reluctance from politician J. Russell Sprague. Sprague, the Nassau GOP leader who created the county executive position he would then occupy, was worried that the construction of Levittown would reduce the number of local Republican voters. In a secret and corrupt patronage deal, he agreed to change zoning laws after arranging for his friends to benefit from important Levittown contracts. Historian Lillian Dudkiewicz-Clayman argues that the influx of Democratic New York City veterans to Levittown caused the Nassau County Republican Party to modernize in an attempt to lure supporters from across the aisle.

William Levitt made Cape Cod– and ranch-style homes affordable to returning veterans. Just $7,990 would buy the original homes, and like teenagers camping out for concert tickets, thousands of people looking for a slice of suburban paradise lined up to purchase them when they became available in March 1949. The development grew to seventeen thousand homes, including sections 16 through 25 in significant parts of East Meadow and Salisbury.

Restrictive covenants, which barred the rental and sale of Levitt homes to African Americans, were deemed ceremoniously unconstitutional in a 1948 Supreme Court case, *Shelley v. Kraemer*. The court unanimously agreed that restrictions were unenforceable in state courts due to the Equal Protection Clause of the Fourteenth Amendment. However, covenants were still legal if private individuals agreed to their terms.

William Levitt claimed to dislike the covenant but saw it as a necessity of doing business in a segregated nation. New Deal programs like the Home Owners Loan Corporation and the Federal Housing Administration supported segregation by using "redlining" techniques—literally drawing red lines around "undesirable" sections of cities—to determine eligibility for mortgages. Returning soldiers buying homes under the G.I. Bill were subject to the same conditions, which created a community that was almost exclusively white. In 1954, one month after the Supreme Court ruled school segregation unconstitutional in *Brown v. Board of Education of Topeka*, Levitt claimed that "the plain fact is that most whites prefer not to live in mixed communities. This attitude may be wrong morally, and some day it may

Levittown under construction. *Nassau County Archives.*

change. I hope it will.…Until it does, it is not reasonable to expect that any builder should or could undertake to absorb the entire risk and burden of conducting such a vast [integration] experiment." By the time he made this statement, Levitt was openly defying the spirit of *Shelley v. Kraemer*. In 1950, Mr. and Mrs. Julius Novic and Mr. and Mrs. Adolph Ross were evicted from their Levitt homes after allowing their own children to play with Black friends on their front lawn. A Committee to End Discrimination in Levittown partnered with the NAACP, the American Jewish Congress and the American Jewish Committee to address discrimination in the development. Although restrictive covenants were definitively outlawed by the Fair Housing Act of 1968, Levittown remained a homogenous community for decades.

In 1949, Levitt began building the more upscale Roslyn Country Club in Roslyn Heights with large home lots that commanded a price more than twice that of Levittown. He ended the rental business and focused solely on home sales. The 1950s—with its new drive-in, television-dominated, keeping-up-with-the-Joneses suburban culture—brought developments with basements, larger homes, bigger plots and garages to East Meadow and its surroundings after the initial Levitt homes were completed. Levitt homes are still beloved by their occupants, who enjoy safe streets, friendly neighbors, good schools and community swimming pools—the embodiment of the American Dream.

Kleindeutschland to Levittown

Levitt built more houses in East Meadow than any other single developer. Eleven sections were planned in 1950 in a German American farming community with heavy marriage ties, traditionally associated with nearby Hicksville. It seems that all the boys literally married the girls next door. Tracing family histories within this community is especially confusing because multiple generations of both boys and girls used their parents' first names. Many of these farmers joined a mutual aid society called des Freundschaftlichen Wohlthätigkeits-Verein, and the local branch met at Charles Kiestling's residence.

Levittown Section 11 (between Twig Lane and Levittown Parkway) was built on the former Henry and Sophia Bartels property, later owned by their children Henry and Frederick. The elder Henry moved to the United States from Germany in 1855 and spent three years fighting in the American Civil War. Frederick lived on Newbridge Road his entire life.

Section 16 ("C" encircled by Cypress Lane) is at the northeast corner of Carman and Stewart Avenues. Most of this section was farmed by the Bremen-born Hohorst family—Diedrich and Anna and then their son Henry, who married Louisa Rowehl of the Bellmore Road German farming community. Their circa 1870 farmhouse still stands. The Rosche and Foley families also had tracts there, and Daniel Hoeffner, elder brother of hotelier Andrew, farmed at the edge of town. Daniel and Anna's daughter Eugenia married Henry Kollmer (of Section 20).

Section 17 ("C" encircled by Choir Lane) is directly opposite, on the northwest corner, previously owned by the Salerno family.

Section 18 ("C" encircled by Cabot Lane) is just south of Section 16, across Stewart Avenue and extending over the town of Oyster Bay line into Hicksville. The land was farmed by August (Jr.) and Margaret Diemicke, whose multiple children married into the Kollmer family (of Section 20). Previously, it had been farmed by Ernest Hartmann and his son Frederick, whose sister Sophia married Henry Bartels (of Section 11).

Section 19 ("F" built around Friends Lane) lies between Carman Avenue and the Wantagh State Parkway. Three related households (Rottkamp and Finn plus Jenny Caruso) lived there in the twentieth century on farms that had previously been in the Laxeng, Heckinger, Wellinghousen, Joseph Berghold, Baker, Henry Bartel and Gasser families. John Gasser, German immigrant and patriarch of that family, lived on various properties at the northeast corner of Carman Avenue and Old Westbury Road with his wife, Mary

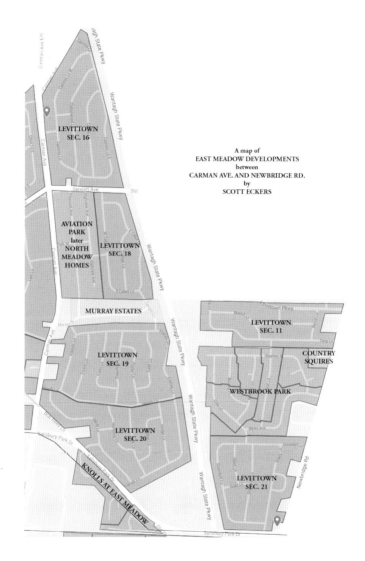

A map of
EAST MEADOW DEVELOPMENTS
between
CARMAN AVE. AND NEWBRIDGE RD.
by
SCOTT ECKERS

Dauch, and their six children. Gasser was the school district's tax collector at the turn of the century. His son and grandson, both named John Gasser, all grew up in the same location. Mary Dauch's father, Nicholas, arrived from Germany in 1845 and settled on Old Westbury Road. Thomas (of Section 20) was Mary's brother.

Section 20 ("H" south of Hearth Lane) lies directly south of Section 19, with an extension of Friends Lane. Thomas and Barbara Dauch and son Adam farmed this land, followed by Henry and Mary Kollmer. Three of their children married Diemicke siblings (of Section 18): Frank married Margaret,

Catherine married Adam and Peter married Mary. Their daughter Anna married William Schneider (son of David, who farmed just north of Section 19) and set up their home next door on the old Henry Schriefer farm. At the corner of Old Westbury Road and Carman Avenue lived John and Wilhelmina Hogrefe, whose daughter Catherine married Henry and Mary's son John Kollmer. Daniel Hoeffner's daughter Eugenia (of Section 16) married Henry Kollmer.

Section 21 ("G" encircled by Greenbelt Lane) lies just across the Wantagh State Parkway, west of Newbridge Road on grounds of the long-standing Adolph and Angelina Pasker estate and New Bridge Hotel. Pasker was one of the earliest German immigrants to come to the New Bridge section. After the Civil War, he was a dairy farmer alongside innkeeper Charles Kiestling. The railroad kept the Hicksville-area milk supply flowing to New York City until prices dropped such that residents could no longer demand enough to be profitable in the 1890s. Pasker became involved with Democratic politics. Gottlieb and Jane Metzger and Jacob Gaenger farmed there before it was sold.

Section 22 ("L") sits at the southwest corner of Stewart Avenue and Carman Avenue.

Section 23 ("M") is situated just south of Section 22's Melody Lane and north of Salisbury Park Drive.

Section 24 ("P" and part of "M") is just west of Section 23, around Palm Lane.

Section 25 ("P" near Pilgrim Lane) lies just west of Section 24 at the intersection of Salisbury Park Drive and Stewart Avenue.

Sections 17 and 22–25 had been part of the vast Hempstead Plains Company holdings, following the nineteenth-century sale of the plains to Alexander Turney Stewart. The posh Meadow Brook Hunt Club, located just west of Merrick Avenue at Stewart Avenue, ran its regular hunts in this section of East Meadow after its 1881 inception. As the plains were developed into suburbia and high society estates were built in the neighborhood, the Meadow Brook Hunt Club shifted its focus to horse racing, then polo and finally golf. When property was taken by the state for the Meadowbrook Parkway extension in 1954, the club moved its headquarters to Jericho. Some of the grounds have been incorporated into Nassau Community College. A Revolutionary-era road to Hicksville ran from Uniondale through the hunt at this location; Old Westbury Road ran northwest through the properties to Old Country Road through the 1920s but now ends at Carman Avenue.

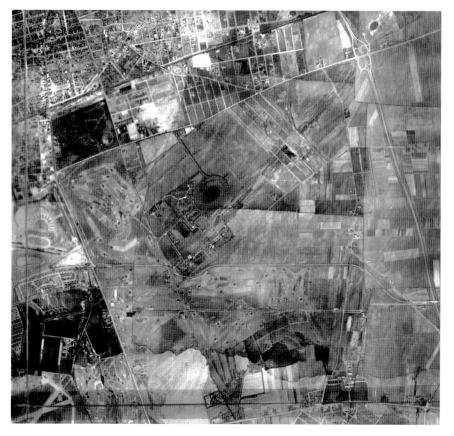

Aerial photo of Salisbury, 1950.

Sections 22 through 25 surround Bowling Green School, which was set aside by Levitt for that purpose. Section 22–23 land was acquired from the Rottkamp family, whose farm homes still stand on Carman Avenue. The Rottkamps were one of the largest families on Long Island; there are more than two thousand descendants of Bernard Rottkamp and Caroline Engel, who wed in New York City in 1851. The family members who remained farmers, children of Henry and Theresa Wulforst Rottkamp, migrated from Elmont to East Meadow in the 1920s. Although they only spent about twenty-five years living in East Meadow, the Rottkamps transformed Carman Avenue: the 1930 federal census lists seven households just with the name Rottkamp living one after another, growing vegetables. A sister, Mary Teresa Rottkamp, lived across the street with her husband, John Finn. The character of New Road, as it was also known, and New Bridge as a German American farming enclave came to a screeching halt in 1950 as the Rottkamps, Schneiders, Gassers and their neighbors—Kollmer, Metzger, Bartels, Finn, Caruso, Nenninger (Pasker) and Diemicke—sold off farms en masse to Levitt.

NEW BRIDGE AND CLEARMEADOW

The New Bridge neighborhood near Old Westbury Road was heavily German for about one hundred years prior to its transformation into suburbia. Several of the families (e.g., Gasser, Dauch and Berg) became related through marriage. This section looks at the properties near Carman Avenue and Newbridge Road that were not sold to Levitt.

The Banchbach family had farmed the corner of Carman and Hempstead (later Stewart) Avenues beginning in the antebellum period. In 1911, the land was purchased by Manhattan Land and Security Company, which mapped out a subdivision called Aviation Park. The name was appropriate, given that the nascent aerospace industry was heralded into its golden age on the Hempstead Plains. Aviation Park never took off. Park Street and Highview and Pleasant Avenues sat vacant until Max Price and Daniel Alterman built North Meadow Homes in 1952, priced at $11,790 and $12,490. Muray Rosenblum built Murray Estates at Murray Drive in 1953 on farmland formerly belonging to David and Anna Schneider. Across the

Louis Schneider Sr. plowing land at 702 Carman Avenue, 1940. *Steve Buczak Collection.*

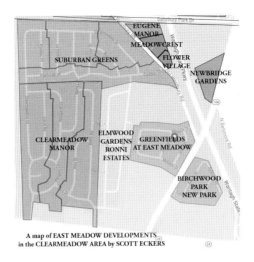

A map of EAST MEADOW DEVELOPMENTS in the CLEARMEADOW AREA by SCOTT ECKERS

street in 1965, East Meadow Estates rose on Rottkamp cousin Ferdinand and Mary Schmitt's homestead.

Clearmeadow Manor was built by Sergei Camp (Chmelnitzky) and his father, Nickolas, in three sections in 1950 and 1951. Houses initially sold for less than $10,000; two hundred were sold the first year. By the time Section 3 opened in 1951, the Meadow, Mainliner and Challenger models were selling for up to $13,950. Birchwood builders Seymour Sadkin and Morris Schoenfeld built Elmwood Gardens in two "Ronni Estates" sections on the former Buck property in 1951 and 1952. Streets were named after Seymour's children Ronni and David and for Morris's daughter Susan. Two Stanley Klein–designed brick center-hall models were the $13,290 Comanche ("All on one floor!") $13,990 Chippewa and Sun Valley Sioux ("Ranch House of the Year contender!"). A four-bedroom model was available for $14,590.

Residents from Clearmeadow Manor and Elmwood Gardens joined to create the Meadow-Wood Civic Association, led by Anthony Lordi and Irving Levine. In 1953, homeowners opposed an adjacent forty-five-acre light industrial area on Sophie Rhodes's estate along Old Westbury Road called Levittown Industrial Terminal, which Morris Sosnow planned to develop alongside homes. This section, beside the LIRR, had been rezoned in 1951; 1,500 residents felt that they were misled into thinking single-family homes would be built there. They hired neighbor-lawyers Nahman and Edith Zirinsky and fought the town board's decision, arguing that the industrial center would cause an increase in traffic and lower property values. They claimed that insufficient notice of a hearing was given. Hundreds of parents and students objected to factories next to new schools

Elmwood Gardens.

under construction. Under immense pressure, the developers had given up by December 1954.

Suburban Greens, planned as Suburban Meadowbrook in 1955, was built by Herman Cooper and Edmund Robbins instead. The 225 identical $15,990 houses newly designed by architect Stanley Shaftel were very stereotypical for the late 1950s: raised living rooms with wrought-iron railings, a hanging light over a high "panoramic" entrance, "duo-rama" bathroom, modern kitchen with built-in appliances, full basement and prominent twenty-four-square curved bay window. The builders highlighted the "unsurpassed location" adjacent to Meadowbrook Elementary and Junior High Schools and easy transportation options to the city and nearby villages. They must have liked cars—all streets are named for automobiles.

Old Westbury Road's Suburban Park Jewish Center was organized in 1958 and built across from the Suburban Greens development in 1962 on property that was once planned as a small development called Eugene Manor. The synagogue was a "breakaway minyan" of ten families from East Meadow Jewish Center, as the latter was not within walking distance. Leadership was Rabbi Morris Schnall, Cantor Nathan Lazow and President Aaron Chaffkin. After many years as a Conservative congregation and merging with Uniondale Jewish Center in 1987, membership dwindled in the early 2000s. The remaining families hired Sam Krasner, an Orthodox rabbi, to lead them until the doors were shuttered in 2019.

Just east sits Meadowcrest and Flower Village, on property that was held by H. Wagner and H. Forstman before the Civil War. Newbridge Gardens was planned in 1988, its property border at an angle with Old Westbury Road's alignment before the completion of the Wantagh State Parkway in 1938. This area had been settled by Danish immigrant Lawrence Jepsen and later Henry Plate. Senior development Knolls of East Meadow was laid out between 1992 and 1996 next to Salisbury Park Drive Ballfields.

The triangle of land bounded by Hempstead Turnpike, Wantagh State Parkway and Newbridge Road—much of which was later commercial development including stores, restaurants and a movie theater—was settled by the Duryea family prior to the Civil War. In 1860, George and Harriet Duryea were living there with their seven children. Fifty years later, Albert and Elizabeth Berg were raising their seven children on the farm. One daughter, Estelle, married William Lowden, of a neighboring prominent family. The land on which Berg raised potatoes and peaches since 1897 slowly diminished. The town rezoned land abutting Hempstead Turnpike and Newbridge Road to "business" in 1948 in anticipation of Berg selling the land to Harvey Newins for the purpose of building stores and Meadowbrook Theatre, which was designed by Edwin Bullock and opened in 1949. Albert Berg died on the property in 1950, after which his last remaining eight acres of farmland were sold for development. The abandoned farmhouse contained turn-of-the-century women's dresses and handwritten letters about exploring the county by buggy during the Teddy Roosevelt years. America on Wheels' Levittown Roller Rink operated there from 1955 to 1986 under Don Victor and George Petrone (with Jahn's ice cream parlor); Rockbottom took over the site after the rink's closure. Just north of the business district at Corey Lane, Morris Sosnow and Leonard Schwartz built thirty-eight "New Park" homes in 1953 and 1954.

The northwest corner of Newbridge Road and Hempstead Turnpike, also included in the 1948 rezoning, became a commercial and recreational center in the 1950s. Samuel Weiss of Salisbury opened Shoe King Sam's flagship store there in 1952, which capitalized on the nation's obsession with cars by featuring a drive-in! The large discount store, along with sixty to seventy thousand pairs of shoes worth about $250,000, burned in 1958. Pascal Lordi opened Pat Lordi's Golf Range there in 1952. He seized on a nationwide trampoline craze shortly thereafter by rebranding part of the range as "Jumpsville, U.S.A." Lordi became the head golf pro at nearby Eisenhower Park between 1970 and 1991, pioneering clinics for women. Together with Edward Speno and David Rothbaum, Lordi founded the East Meadow Chamber of Commerce and Kiwanis Club. He became a kingpin in local Republican politics, striking deals and making party decisions over golf. The Republican Party/East Meadow Chamber of Commerce/ Kiwanis Club interaction has remained strong, and membership rolls of the three organizations have traditionally overlapped.

Pat Lordi's gave way to Great Eastern Mills, which operated from 1969 to 1975. When it was proposed in 1966, residents from the Clearmeadow area opposed construction of such a large store by picketing at town hall; when it opened, however, the discount center was flooded with excited shoppers. F.W. Woolworth's operated Woolco Plaza Shopping Center

Left: Mrs. Berg on the family farm, October 1918. *Steve Buczak Collection.*

Above: Pat Lordi's, 1955. *Sherman Collection of Jeffrey Rosen.*

there from 1978 to 1983, at which time it was turned into Clearmeadow Mall, with Service Merchandise as its anchor. Reflecting the character of the adjacent neighborhood, a yearly matzo factory and kosher-for-Passover superstore operated in Mel Weitz's Foodtown. The enclosed mall was rebuilt as a Walmart in 2001 (returning, in a way, to its Great Eastern roots), with several tenants moving to their own buildings. Greenfields of East Meadow was built just north in 1988, following demolition of McCleary Junior High School.

With its entrance at Myles Avenue, Westbrook Park was built by father-and-son team Louis and Jack Desner in six sections of "Newbridge Acres" between 1953 and 1955. Pasquale and Gelsomina De Monaco had previously lived there, but the area was settled by Joshua Pink in the nineteenth century and later John and Mary Elfing and Joseph and Mary Essling. Split-level homes with finished recreation and hobby rooms designed by architect Abraham Harold Salkowitz sold for $14,990 to $16,990. Salkowitz was a significant force in the development of suburban New York—first in Queens and then in Nassau—responsible for more than ten thousand housing units. He was notable for designing the Levittown Center shopping plaza in 1950, then the nation's largest. Three years later, he designed the East Meadow Shopping Center at Front Street and Merrick Avenue, anchored by Food

Newbridge Road and Hempstead Turnpike, eastbound, 1938. *Nassau County Highway Department.*

Fair—the scene of infamous and unsolved kidnapping of one-year-old Steven Damman in 1955. Salkowitz later designed synagogues and the North Shore Towers complex on the Queens border. A small Country Squires cul-de-sac was added in 1964 on property adjacent to Westbrook Park.

SALISBURY

During the Gilded Age, Westbury emerged as a center of high society living. Meadow Brook Park was home to ladies and gentlemen involved with foxhunting and equestrianism. Suburban developers capitalized on the name to appeal to buyers. Since Salisbury's overlapping services include some with the name Westbury, real estate agents played along. In the days of Rural Free Delivery, the Stewart Avenue area got its mail from Westbury. Confusion over location spilled over into controversy when Mary Louise Clarke, wife of school leader W. Tresper, accused Herman Schwartz of misrepresenting his development as being in Westbury Village. Meadow Brook Colony, located at the corner of Old Country Road and Newbridge Avenue, was the earliest subdivision. Although streets were opened in 1915, most lots remained empty.

Joseph Gross developed Bowling Green Estates in 1927. Seeing value in the Hempstead Plains, Gross purchased native prairie grassland and advertised heavily, stressing its location on an extension of Garden City's "famous" Stewart Avenue and the thrill of nearby Curtiss, Roosevelt and Mitchel Fields: "It is ideally situated to share in the prosperity that the aeroplane will bring." Gross envisioned owners building country estates

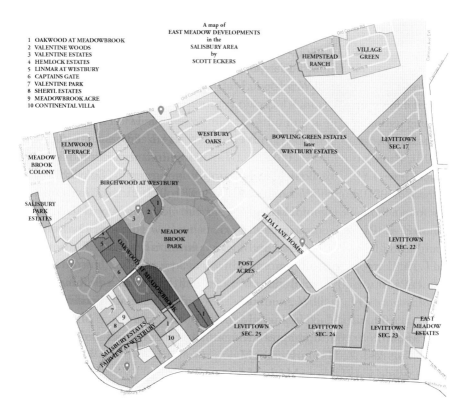

1 OAKWOOD AT MEADOWBROOK
2 VALENTINE WOODS
3 VALENTINE ESTATES
4 HEMLOCK ESTATES
5 LINMAR AT WESTBURY
6 CAPTAINS GATE
7 VALENTINE PARK
8 SHERYL ESTATES
9 MEADOWBROOK ACRE
10 CONTINENTAL VILLA

A map of
EAST MEADOW DEVELOPMENTS
in the
SALISBURY AREA
by
SCOTT ECKERS

on wide streets, but it was not to be. A few homes were built on Merillon Avenue and Myron Road in the 1930s, which were improved with sidewalks and shrubbery. Like with his other East Meadow projects, most of the land remained bare, and lots were sold to later developers during the early baby boom period. The five-hundred-family neighborhood was built as Westbury Estates by Herman Schwartz beginning in 1948. The homes were approved by the FHA and initially priced just below $10,000, appealing to working-class veterans. FHA also insured the adjacent forty-seven-unit Hempstead Ranch Homes (around Aster Place), selling for $13,500 and featuring combination living/dining room and V-shaped "Hollywood kitchens." That year, board of education president William Schindel asked taxpayers to approve a ten-acre site for the construction of a Bowling Green School. Until it was completed in 1952, the district contemplated sending students to nearby Westbury. Growth was so fast that the tuition would have been unsustainable. Instead, East Meadow bused a few hundred students to Front Street and then Prospect Avenue schools. Residents organized a civic association, which aligned with the Protective League.

Fairview-at-Westbury (Salisbury Estates) was built by David Strausman on the former Ladenburg/Davie estate in 1952. Three-bedroom center-hall ranches designed by Rudolph Matern and Herman York started at $18,990 and included wood-burning fireplaces. Each sat on an oversized suburban lot. Morris Strow and Emanuel Rosenberg built Oakwood at Meadowbrook (1955–58) surrounding the old Boelsen home, encompassing a significant portion of Meadow Brook Park on both sides of Valentines and The Plain Roads.

Birchwood at Westbury was built by Herbert and Seymour "Sy" Sadkin and Morris Schoenfeld in eight sections between 1952 and 1955 on old Meadow Brook Park colony estates. About 450 homes around Birchwood, Stratford, Roxbury, Bromton and Regent Drives were priced at $23,000, with "unusual" features for Brick splits: open balconies and large Cathedral-style living rooms. Sadkin also built the adjacent Elmwood Terrace around Meryl Drive in 1957. Westbury Oaks, encircled by Edgewood Drive just east of Birchwood, was built by Saul, David and Samuel Janowitz and Louis Entman of Woodcliff Building Organization in 1955. At $23,990, the two hundred brick and stone-faced split-level homes by Alwin Cassens Jr. were costly compared to those in neighboring Bowling Green. The final small developments in the Meadow Brook Park Ladenburg/Boelsen area were Meadowbrook Acre (1955), Continental Villa (1963), Valentine Park (1964) and Sheryl Estates (1971).

On the former Ellis estate north of Valentines Road, Alan Fox, Malcolm Hecker and Herbert Gold built a cul-de-sac called Valentine Estates in 1961. Stratford Park Company's Valentine Woods followed in 1964. David Tishman's Captains Gate rose on a cul-de-sac to the west in 1967.

"Rancher" homes by architects Schuman and Lichtenstein in Post Acres (around Plum Tree Road), developed by Edward Eadiekis and Monte Egeloff in 1951–52, featured three bedrooms, garage, basement and expansion attic. Advertisements boasted that the $10,990 price tag included four appliances. Veterans paid only $550 down. Irving Steinberg built Elda Lane (Long Island) Homes in 1951. The $11,990 to $12,490 "High, Wide and Handsome" Cape Cods by architect William La Valle incorporated "all the ultra-modern space-saving features." Several farmhouses were retained from Charles Crowley, on whose property these developments were built. In 1953, Steinberg built Village Green around Hyacinth Lane.

So many families flooded the new developments that schools, already overwhelmed, were now forced to house part-time classes for all students. In advance of an October 1953 "package" $3,510,000 school expansion

Birchwood.

Temple Sholom. *Temple Sholom.*

referendum, Salisbury's children paraded neighborhood streets, urging voters to approve the plan. Civic associations and even the typically hesitant Protective League voiced their support.

The neighborhood, with its then-trendy "South" Westbury postal addresses, was developed principally by Jews who championed Jewish causes. Temple Sholom, the Birchwood Jewish Center, was built squarely within the Sadkin and Schoenfeld development on land they donated. The first members met in a tent in 1955 with East Meadow Democratic Club chairman Max Goldweber as president. Resident "Shoe King" Samuel Weiss donated money to help erect a building two years later. According to founding member William Kavee, Weiss also helped negotiate a deal in which Franklin Bank would grant a mortgage if enough congregants opened accounts. The first permanent rabbi, Maurice Aranov, was a Korean War veteran seeking his first job. Cantor Sol Zim served the four-hundred-member congregation.

A TRIANGLE OF COMMERCE

Ah, the bustling commerce, and traffic, in the triangle that sits neatly at the intersection of Hempstead Turnpike, Front Street and East Meadow Avenue. Prior to becoming back-to-back shopping centers, the "triangle" was an elaborate agricultural operation. In 1927, Otto Muller Florist began operating on the land. One of Muller's workers, Kurt Weiss, subsequently married Muller's daughter Lena in 1934. Together, Weiss and Muller worked the land and expanded the property to twenty-three acres. In 1960, the business became known as Kurt Weiss Florist, and a home was built at the corner of Front Street and Newbridge Avenue. After Kurt's son Russell took over the business and moved it to Center Moriches, the properties were converted to the current shopping plazas. All the old buildings were demolished in April 1968. The Weiss family retained the northern parcel facing Hempstead Turnpike, which was sold for $25.6 million in 2007.

In 1970, when the northern property at 1900 Hempstead Turnpike was developed, records show twenty-four businesses (from east to west): AMP Savings Bank, Shir Center, Shoe Town, Paul Stewart, sport wear, men's shop, record shop, theater, professional suites, dress store, corset shop, hairdresser, barber, hosiery, bakery, pizza, VAC, fabric, stationery, Allied Radio, repair, travel agency, scalp shop and Magnavox. Some of the same types of businesses are there today, even in the same locations! A later business, Penrod's, was the first major dance club on Long Island during the height of the disco craze. Penrod's later became Zachary's Nightclub.

Perhaps you tried out the echo chamber leading to the shopping center facing Front Street, continuing into the little interior mall with PathMark, a homage to awkward silvery-dome 1980s architecture. When the property was remodeled at the beginning of that decade, East Meadow residents

Kurt Weiss, florist. *Weiss.*

could also visit Channel Hardware, Satellite Stores and the American Savings Bank. This property was redeveloped by Stew Leonard's.

While Kurt Weiss was still growing flowers, Ann Yeni's 2000 Hempstead Turnpike developed into Modell's Shoppers World, a discount retail center and supermarket. The building was erected in 1956, remodeled in 1963 and then enlarged in 1970 when the adjacent property was developed. Modell's ended its run as a sporting goods chain sharing space with Home Depot and was removed in 2020. Who can forget White Castle, the one-hour photo booth in the middle of the parking lot or the neat little police booth nearby?

HATE CRIMES CHALLENGE VIEWPOINTS

The earliest known Black family in East Meadow was that of Eliakim and Martha Levi (and later their son Charles and Margaret Levi), who lived on Newbridge Avenue just south of Old Country Road. Eliakim was the first minister of New Light Baptist Church (later Westbury AME Zion Church, founded 1834) for Guinea Town, a settlement of freed slaves near Westbury. The Levis lived next to impressive Salisbury estates and had a servant, but for years they worked for the Hicks family and were socially and economically tied to the nearby Quaker community, which supported manumission and the Underground Railroad.

Through the baby boom period, East Meadow was about 98 percent white. The few Black families were generally stationed at Mitchel AFB. A 1962 meeting of the new East Meadow Committee for Human Rights explored the problems of living in a segregated suburban society. Most of the participants came in support of equal housing rights, but several vocal attendees voiced concern that such "mixing" would lead to intermarriage and ghettoization.

In 1963, biracial couple Vincent and Tamara Wright moved to Marlboro Street in an all-white, conservative section of East Meadow. Vincent asked the seller if the neighborhood would be okay, and he was told there hadn't ever been a problem. He moved in with some trepidation. At first, the music teacher and his wife were popular with a small group, but they soon found themselves targets of vandalism and telephone and mail threats. Others ignored them completely. On June 27, 1965, a seven-foot-high cross was burned on their lawn in an apparent hate crime. Police who responded extinguished the fire and called it a youthful prank.

Committee for Human Rights president Jerry Silverman called the incident a "Ku Klux Klan–like act of lawlessness." Ten days later, firecrackers taped to their windows exploded and broke panes of glass while the Wrights' children slept nearby. Silverman demanded police protection for the interracial household, vowing to organize a parade in support of the family. Careful detective work led to the arrest of teenagers Clifford Snyder, James Kaylor and a fifteen-year-old for malicious mischief in the firecracker incident, and Vincent Dantone Jr. and Mark Sanko for disorderly conduct for their role in "outraging public decency" by burning a cross. Most were East Meadow High School students. Although Snyder and Kaylor said they took aim at "the colored man's house" and Dantone and Sanko said, "Let's burn a cross on the lawn of the colored fellow," police chose not to pursue civil rights charges. Still, Silverman praised the police work and called off the march at the Wrights' request. A politically charged meeting of community leaders at the end of July ended with a call to organize programs aimed at "Negro acceptance." The hate crimes were covered widely and featured in *Ebony* magazine that October.

On August 22, 1989, twenty-year-old white man Keith Verdon beat fourteen-year-old Black Hempstead residents David Evans and Gerald Galbreath with a golf club near Figarelly's Deli on East Meadow Avenue. Five teenagers, including Evans and Galbreath, had played basketball at Veterans Memorial Park. Evans had gone into the deli, and the remaining four waited outside. Verdon, who lived across the street, came outside to check why the youths were in his neighborhood. The boys and an independent witness, James Launonen, heard Verdon call them a racial slur while chasing them before beating Evans in the head, chest and arms with a golf club. Launonen stopped to assist Evans, who was seriously hurt.

A few weeks later, on Labor Day, the Hempstead NAACP organized a peaceful march near the crime scene. Seventy marchers showed up.

Wright family, 1965. *From* Ebony.

About fifty counterprotesters stood outside East Meadow Dairy, wearing white supremacist "National White Resistance" shirts and "KKK" drawn on their bodies with markers. They shouted, "N-----s, go home" while holding watermelons, a common racist symbol of Jim Crow America. Police seized a cache of baseball bats from the group. Most counterprotesters

NAACP protest, 1989. *Alan Hlavenka, from* Newsday.

were in their late teens and early twenties, and some were open about their convictions. John Lippiello was upset that "someone gets beat up and they come marching through our neighborhood." Chris Apostolou thought that East Meadow was a safe place for Black people to visit but added, "We just don't want n-----s marching through here." Others, including teenagers and United Methodist Church's Reverend David Parker, defended the marchers and praised their peaceful protest, hoping that it would open minds and lead to racial harmony. Dairy owner Ernest Hatzelman called the police and told reporters, "This is a very good community, and I didn't like those people being out here, not one bit."

In a December trial, the jury found Verdon guilty of criminal possession of a weapon but not guilty of assault and harassment, essentially clearing him of the racial discrimination charge. Verdon leaned on the "Black friend" defense. The jury believed his story that he thought the youngsters were there to steal bicycles and break into his car and that Evans got hurt when falling into lawn stakes, a claim debunked by medical examiner Lone Thanning. Following his acquittal, Verdon stormed out of the courtroom, making a vulgar gesture to those present. The Hempstead community was upset by the verdict, and Detective Mike Herts was surprised at the jury's decision. He believed that the evidence against Verdon was clear but contended that it was difficult to prove racial motivation. He did, however, comment, "Would he have bothered to take the golf club after five white kids? I doubt it." Hempstead NAACP president Barbara Powell believed the jury tacitly approved of Verdon's behavior, leading to an expansion of acceptable hate crimes. For the lesser charge, Verdon was sentenced to probation and ninety days' home detention. Evans's parents sued for $9.5 million relief from civil rights violations.

In response, the nearly all-white East Meadow community tried to paint a portrait of residents differently than those seen on television. Figarelly's owner Wayne Falk remarked, "I'm not saying there isn't some prejudice, but overall this is a good community." That type of post-incident realization seemed to prompt soul-searching among local groups. A group of white residents and clergymen formed an organization to connect residents to their neighbors in Hempstead. Rabbi Ronald Androphy thought that the attack was an aberration but joined his fellow religious leaders of the Clergy Fellowship, saying, "East Meadow is not a racist community. At the same time, it must be acknowledged that all here is not well." The following year, the fellowship united in support of the establishment of a group home for mentally ill residents. When hundreds showed up to oppose the home, religious leaders spoke of the moral duty to accept struggling neighbors.

TEMPLE EMANU-EL

In June 2019, East Meadow lost a significant architectural landmark: Temple Emanu-El. For its members, friends and just those who enjoyed the creative structure, the loss truly hit home, as the synagogue was part of being "home" in East Meadow for sixty-eight years.

East Meadow's first synagogue was Temple Emanu-El. Its founding came on the heels of the 1950 LIRR wreck on Thanksgiving Eve, November 22, 1950, when two trains collided near Kew Gardens, Queens. Seventy-eight commuters were killed in Long Island's worst rail disaster. One of these victims was Emanuel Frankfort, who lived on Argyle Road in East Meadow. Realizing that a need existed for a local synagogue, mourners in the shiva house decided to form a congregation. It is interesting to note that the inevitable need to bury the dead is how most Jewish communal organizations were created around the turn of the century, when millions of immigrants poured into New York City. Patterns of settlement change, but human needs remain.

Emanu-El means "God is with us" but was also a way of remembering Mr. Frankfort. Members of the new Reform congregation first met in homes, the firehouse and a tent. The first president was Joseph Greenberg, the first rabbi was Eugene Lipsey and the first permanent cantor was Lawrence Harwood. The membership purchased Edwin and Lydia Mersereau's large old home on Merrick Avenue, south of Hempstead Turnpike, to use as its house of worship. As this structure was inadequate for the needs of the growing organization, a new synagogue was built in 1956. One year later, the design firm Davis, Brody, and Wisniewski created the iconic circular sanctuary that defined Temple Emanu-El for decades. A product of the Midcentury Modern architectural school, it was featured in a 1963 exhibit called "Recent American Synagogue Architecture" at the Jewish Museum. The original sanctuary was turned into a large auditorium, where locals fondly remember seeing its community theater performances and playing bingo. Another extension was added in 1984. When the 1957 "Beehive" was deemed no longer structurally sound, services were moved once again to the original sanctuary.

A combination of structural issues and a declining membership rate forced Temple Emanu-El to close its doors in June 2018. The congregation merged with Wantagh's Temple B'nai Torah, formerly Suburban Temple.

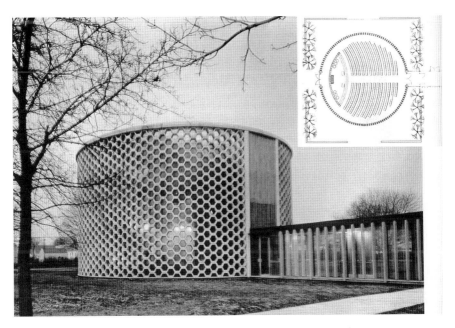

Architect's rendering of Temple Emanu-El. *Samuel Gruber's Jewish Art & Monuments.*

The property was sold to Beechwood, which knocked down the structure in only a few days in May 2019 and began constructing Meadowbrook Pointe senior housing in 2020.

The last spiritual leader of the shul was Rabbi Daniel Bar-Nahum. Prior to his tenure, Albert Lowenberg led the congregation. On June 10, 2018, congregants met for the last time and took a 3.8-mile walk with the Torahs to their new home on Jerusalem Avenue on the Wantagh–North Bellmore border. This bittersweet event followed the congregation's last community theater production of the Broadway classic *Fiddler on the Roof*, in which the final number was staged so that leaving Anatevka was akin to leaving East Meadow. There wasn't a dry eye in the house.

EATING, HISTORICALLY

The East Meadow Hotel (Noon Inn, Schultze Hotel, Andrew Hoeffner Hotel), located on the current Prospect Pool property, was the "center of town" for much of the nineteenth century. It featured a beautiful bar where travelers stopped and locals enjoyed themselves. The other location of interest was the inn on the Carman-Lowden homestead. The Carmans, residing in the town of Hempstead since its seventeenth-century inception, managed the only inn on the Hempstead-Bethpage Turnpike, which ran to Farmingdale. At a time when it could take an entire day to journey out to Long Island from New York City, east–west travelers would stop there for a bite to eat and a good night's rest. In the early twentieth century, spectators enjoying the thrilling Vanderbilt Cup Races would patronize the inn as well.

On Newbridge Avenue, The Keyhole restaurant opened in a building that once held the Polish-influenced Gniewek's Deli. The Keyhole later became Dr. Generosity's, which was a local hangout for New York Islanders fans. Today, Majors Steak House operates in the same building.

For those seeking a hamburger instead of a steak, the earliest fast-food joint was the Fortress (White Fortress Restaurant), owned by Berkley Andrews. This drive-up midcentury restaurant had the slogan "Fortify Yourself" and served burgers, sodas, frozen custard and seafood sandwiches. Berkley and his father, Arthur, established the small chain in 1940. Arthur, who was a Village of Mineola trustee, became widely known as "Pop." The oddly shaped property, purchased from the Lowden estate, became Mr. Donut, which was demolished in 2019.

When I spoke to dozens, if not hundreds, of East Meadow baby boomers, one fast-food restaurant came up over and over again: Dave Shor's, run by David and Arthur Shor. Dave Shor's, like the Fortress, opened in 1949. It was a drive-in at the corner of Hempstead Turnpike and Merrick Avenue and quickly became a popular spot for neighborhood youngsters. The restaurant claimed it was "Shor" to satisfy hungry customers with its typical American fare. It lasted until 1976.

Across from Dave Shor's, the Central Island Restaurant opened before 1950. By that time, Hempstead Turnpike was growing into a major thoroughfare with prime real estate for commercial establishments. In 1955, the three Borrelli brothers purchased Central Island and converted it into the Italian restaurant that thrives to this day. Business grew so quickly that large additions to the structure were completed in 1962.

One cannot speak of eating on Long Island without mentioning diners, and East Meadow has had its share! Milteades Galanes ran an older establishment called the Meadowbrook Diner (originally Meadow Brook Grill, also called Pop's Place) until 1959 at the northeast corner of Hempstead Turnpike and Newbridge Road. The Levitt family would frequent the diner when building Levittown. Just east at Levittown Roller Rink was Jahn's, a franchise of a small chain of ice cream parlors where one could order the "Kitchen Sink." In the '50s and '60s, mom and pop luncheonettes ruled in East Meadow. Schoolchildren, allowed to leave for lunch, took advantage. The Empress Diner opened across the street in 1955 and was run from 1967 until 2018 by the Panagatos family. The Stardust Diner opened in 1966 and is now known as the Colony Diner. Finally, the Apollo Diner on Merrick Avenue began operating in 1967. Each diner was remodeled throughout the years, following fires and the latest restaurant trends. The last long-standing family establishment was Wayne Falk's Figarelly's Deli.

A popular Italian restaurant near Sabia's Corner was the Orchard Tavern, run by Max Scafidi (aka Michael Scafford). For eastern European fare, East Meadow residents could visit Brodie's Kosher Delicatessen, which was a staple in the Mitchel Manor Shopping Plaza. There one could order a tongue on rye and a Dr. Brown's soda!

Roads through the Meadow

Here is key information regarding names changes of major thoroughfares through East Meadow:

Merrick Avenue: Whaleneck Road (realigned/straightened between 1873 and 1882), Barnum Avenue

Bellmore Avenue: Westbury Road

East Meadow Avenue: Newbridge Avenue, Bellmore-Westbury Road, Westbury Road, road from Westbury to Newbridge and, rarely or inconsistently, Smithville South Road

Newbridge Road: New Bridge Path, road from Jericho to Newbridge, Hicksville Road (north of Hempstead Turnpike)

Salisbury Park Drive (east–west section): Long Island Motor Parkway, County Road

Old Westbury Road (included Bob Reed Lane and originally ran to Old Country Road): Jerusalem Road, Westbury to Jerusalem Road, Gasser Avenue

Carman Avenue: New Road

Stewart Avenue (east of Carman Avenue): Hempstead Avenue, Dutch Lane (for the Dauch family)

Hempstead Turnpike: Hempstead-Bethpage Turnpike, Bethpage Turnpike, Bethpage Road, Hempstead-Farmingdale Turnpike, Fulton Street, Fulton Avenue

Front Street: Barnum Avenue

Prospect Avenue: Hay Carter's Lane and, rarely or inconsistently, West Road, Sleepy Lane or Fisher's Avenue

North Jerusalem Road: Jerusalem Road, Jerusalem Avenue North (was current-day Spencer Avenue and Ennabrock Road before 1950 realignment), road to Hempstead

Wilson Road: Christian Road

Macadamization (paving with crushed stones) of Hempstead Turnpike to East Meadow occurred in 1896. Initial paving of other main roads through East Meadow took place through the next decade, including Newbridge Avenue in 1906. The early decades of the twentieth century saw the closure of colonial-era roads that ran through the Hempstead Plains. The Revolutionary-era "Old Cart Path" to Hicksville that originated at Hempstead Turnpike west of Merrick Avenue was closed in segments. A tiny stretch of that road connects Stewart Avenue from its original end at Old Westbury Road (in front of today's Bowling Green School) to its current terminus at Newbridge Road. In the late 1920s, Old Westbury Road (Westbury to Jerusalem Road) was truncated and now ends at Carman Avenue.

Hempstead Turnpike and Newbridge Road, showing Clearmeadow area, Pat Lordi's, Meadowbrook Theatre and Meadowbrook School (under construction); Wantagh State Parkway is on the right with Levittown, 1954. *Author's collection.*

In 1947, the Town of Hempstead began a renumbering system in unincorporated areas, spearheaded by Carroll McLaughlin. The new uniform address system would make it easier to find buildings, deliver mail and promote safety by allowing first responders to find emergencies faster. Every twenty feet, the minimum allowed lot size, the address would increase by two. Most lots are sixty feet wide; therefore, most houses in East Meadow have addresses that are six numbers apart. Hempstead Turnpike is the "0" line for north–south addresses, and the intersection of Hempstead Turnpike and Front Street at the western edge of the Village of Hempstead is the "0" line for east–west addresses. Developments planned after 1947 adopted the new system before homes on established streets were changed after 1950. Several streets were renamed to avoid confusion over duplicates.

Nassau County fenced in the County Park at Salisbury (later Eisenhower Park) in 1947 so it could control who had access to the golf courses. In doing so, remaining roads running through the park (Sprague Avenue and parts of Newbridge and Stewart Avenues) were closed. The north–south section of Salisbury Park Drive was once connected to East Meadow Avenue, which is why midcentury maps show both sections as Newbridge Avenue.

The Newbridge Avenue name change (to East Meadow Boulevard, as originally suggested) was proposed by Town Councilman Gregory Peterson and supported by chamber of commerce members so people could more easily find businesses, but it was opposed by many residents. First responders were also concerned about response times to emergencies because of the confusion over Newbridge Road and Newbridge Avenue. The renaming to East Meadow Avenue took effect on May 28, 1982.

Selected Bibliography

American Builder. "Splits Levels on Parade" (1953): 74–76.

Ancestry.com. https://www.ancestry.com.

Atlas of Nassau County, Long Island, N.Y. Brooklyn, NY: E. Belcher-Hyde, 1906, 1914, 1927.

Bailey, Paul. "Historic Long Island." *The Wave,* October 10, 1957.

Bayles, Richard M. *Bayles' Long Island Handbook.* Babylon, NY: Budget Steam Print, 1885.

Beers, F.W. *Map of Long Island.* New York: Beers, Comstock & Cline, 1873.

Bellmore Life. 1974, 2010.

Brooklyn Citizen. 1887–1926.

Brooklyn (Daily) Eagle. 1873–1955.

Brooklyn Daily Times/Times-Union. 1872–1935.

Burnett, General Ward B. *Report of the Water Committee of the City of Brooklyn.* Brooklyn, NY: I. Van Anden's Press, 1854.

Cassens, Alwin, Jr. *Ranch Homes for Today.* New York: Archway Press, 1953.

Clarke, Mary Louise. *East Meadow: Its History, Our Heritage.* East Meadow, NY, 1952.

Day, Lynda R. "Friends in the Spirit: African Americans and the Challenge to Quaker Liberalism, 1776–1915." *Long Island Historical Journal* 10, 1 (1998): 1–16.

Derry, Margaret E. *Bred for Perfection.* Baltimore, MD: Johns Hopkins University Press, 2003.

Dolph's Street, Road and Land Ownership Map of Nassau County, Long Island, New York. New York: Dolph & Stewart, 1939.

East Meadow Community Concerts Association v. Board of Education of Union Free School District No. 3, County of Nassau. 224 N.E.2d 888. Court of Appeals of the State of New York, January 19, 1967.

East Meadow Public Library. *East Meadow: Its Past and Present, 1858–1976.* East Meadow, NY: self-published, 1976.

Eckers, Scott M. *East Meadow.* Charleston, SC: Arcadia Publishing, 2016.

Edwards and Critten, eds. *New York's Great Industries: Exchange and Commercial Review, Embracing also Historical and Descriptive Sketch of the City, Its Leading Merchants and Manufacturers.* New York: Historical Publishing Company, 1885.

Emory, Ester, et al. *Westbury History in Stride.* Westbury, NY: Historical Society of the Westburys, 2007.

Encyclopedia Titanica. "James Clinch Smith." 2004. https://www.encyclopedia-titanica.org/james-clinch-smith.html.

Evans, Colin. *Valentino Affair: The Jazz Age Murder Scandal that Shocked New York Society and Gripped the World.* Lanham, MD: Rowman & Littlefield, 2014.

Fish, John Dean. "History and Vital Records of Christ's First Presbyterian Church of Hempstead, Long Island, N.Y." In *New York Genealogical and Biographical Record.* New York: New York Genealogical and Biographical Society, 1922.

Flint, Marthan Bockée. *Early Long Island: A Colonial Study.* New York: G.P. Putnam's Sons, 1896.

(Freeport) Daily Review. 1923–1925.

George A. Mott Against Emma H. Mott. 524. New York Supreme Court, Appellate Division—Second Department, February 20, 1907.

Goldblatt et al. v. Town of Hempstead. 369. U.S. Supreme Court, May 14, 1962.

Graham, Hugh Davis. "The Paradox of Eleanor Roosevelt: Alcoholism's Child." *Virginia Quarterly Review* 63, no. 2 (2013). https://www.vqronline.org/essay/paradox-eleanor-roosevelt-alcoholism%E2%80%99s-child.

"Hempstead Census." 1698. Hempstead, New York. http://sites.rootsweb.com/~nynassa2/census.htm.

Hempstead Sentinel. 1900–1934.

Hicks, Benjamin D., ed. *Records of the Towns of North and South Hempstead.* Vol. 4. Jamaica, NY: Long Island Farmer Print, 1900.

Holland, Evangeline. "Sin and Scandal: The de Saulles Murder Case." Edwardian Promenade, September 26, 2013. http://www.edwardianpromenade.com/crime/sin-and-scandal-the-de-saulles-murder-case.

House & Home. "People" (January 1954): 52.

House of Representatives, Congress, Committee on Un-American Activities. "Investigation of Communist Activities, New York Area (Entertainment): Hearings, 84th Congress." *History Matters*, August 18, 1955. historymatters. gmu.edu/d/6457.

Johnson, John H., ed. "The Trials of an Interracial Couple." *Ebony* (October 1965): 66–75.

Kadinsky, Sergey. "East Meadow Brook, Merrick." *Hidden Waters*, October 28, 2019. https://hiddenwatersblog.wordpress.com/2019/10/28/meadowbrook.

Kelly, Barbara M. *Expanding the American Dream: Building and Rebuilding Levittown.* Albany: State University of New York, 1993.

Kroplick, Howard. "New Bridge Hotel on Newbridge Road." Vanderbilt Cup Races, February 15, 2016. https://www.vanderbiltcupraces.com/blog/article/mystery_friday_foto_7_a_favorite_viewing_site_for_three_vanderbilt_cup_race.

Linder, Douglas O., ed. "Testimony of James Clinch Smith, Stanford White's Brother-in-Law." 1907. Famous Trials. http://famous-trials.com/thaw/431-smithtestimony.

Long Island Black and White Aerials Collection—Nassau County, 1938. Stony Brook University Libraries Digital Research Collections. August 3. http://digital.library.stonybrook.edu/cdm/landingpage/collection/aerial.

Long Island Chamber of Commerce. *Long Island: "The Sunrise Homeland."* New York: Schwarzbach Publishing Corporation, 1928.

Long Islander. 1896–1917.

Long Island Farmer (and Queens County Advertiser). 1822–1908.

Long Island Herald. 2001–15.

Long Island Star-Journal. 1950–53.

Long Island Sunday Press. 1935.

Macdonald, Alastair. "Minutes of Meeting of Board of Education of Union Free School District No. 3." East Meadow, NY: East Meadow Union Free School District No. 3, 1952.

Map of Long Island. Brooklyn, NY: Hyde & Company, 1897.

Map of Long Island East to Ronkonkoma. Brooklyn: Hyde & Company, 1896.

Map of Queens and Nassau Counties. New York: Hagstrom, 1946.

Mourning Courier and New-York Enquirer. 1845.

Nassau County Land Records, 2021. http://i2f.uslandrecords.com/NY/Nassau.

Nassau County Review. 1908–14.

Nassau County, New York. "History of Eisenhower Park." 2011. https://www.nassaucountyny.gov/4246/History-of-Eisenhower-Park.

———. "Nassau County 1950 Aerial Photography." 1950. Nassau County, New York. https://gis.nassaucountyny.gov/arcgis/rest/services/Aerial_1950/ImageServer.

Nassau Daily Review/Review-Star. 1926–62.

New Map of Kings and Queens Counties, New York. New York: J.B. Beers & Company, 1886.

Newsday. 1940–2019.

Newtown Register. 1887–93.

New York (Daily) Tribune. 1887–1921.

New York Herald Tribune. 1953.

New York Journal and Advertiser. 1899.

New York Post. 1951–58.

New York Press. 1891.

New York State Census. 1905, 1915, 1925.

New York Times. 1894–2018.

Poliakoff, Ira. *Synagogues of Long Island*. Charleston, SC: The History Press, 2017.

Queens County Review. 1898.

Queens County Sentinel. 1858–97.

Real Estate Reference Map of Nassau County, Long Island. New York: E. Belcher-Hyde, 1923.

Ross, Peter. *A History of Long Island: From Its Earliest Settlement to the Present Time*. New York: Lewis Publishing Company, 1902.

Rudin, A. James, and Marcia R. Rudin. "Onward (Hebrew) Christian Soldiers." *Present Tense* 4, no. 4 (1977): 17–26.

Schaefer, Richard. *Phase 1A Archaeological Assessment—Nassau County Health Care Corporation*. Archaeological Assessment. Westport, CT: Historical Perspectives Inc., 2009.

Social Register Association. *Dilatory Domiciles*. New York: Social Register Association, 1913.

South Side Observer. 1880–1916.

Spinzia, Raymond E. "Elliott Roosevelt, Sr.—A Spiral Into Darkness: The Influences." *The Freeholder* 12 (2007): 3–7, 15–17.

Spinzia, Raymond E., and Judith A. Spinzia. *Long Island's Prominent Families in the Town of Hempstead: Their Estates and Their Country Homes*. College Station, TX: VirtualBookworm, 2010.

Sprague, J. Russel. *A Nassau County Park at Salisbury*. Mineola, NY: Nassau County, 1944.

Tabler, Judith. *Foxhunting with Meadow Brook*. New York: Derrydale Press, 2016.

———. "Theodore Roosevelt Conflicted: Fox Hunting on Long Island." *Theodore Roosevelt Institute Centenary Conference.* Brookville, NY: Long Island University, 2019.

Tanaka, Denise Robarge. *The Killing of John L. de Saulles.* November 30, 2020. https://jackdesaulles.blogspot.com.

Town of Hempstead v. Goldblatt. 9 N.Y. 2d 101. Court of Appeals of the State of New York, January 19, 1961.

United Methodist Church. *A Look Backward….* East Meadow, NY: self-published, 1984.

U.S. Congress. "East Meadow Good Neighbors Meeting." Congressional Record: Proceedings and Debates of the 89th Congress—House, Washington, D.C., 1965.

U.S. Federal Census. 1790–1880, 1900–1940.

Van Alystne, Henry A. *Annual Report of the State Engineer and Surveyor of the State of New York.* Albany, NY: Brandow Printing Company, 1905.

Van Wagenen, Jared. *Century Farms of New York State.* New York: New York Telephone Company, 1947.

Walling, Henry Francis. *Topographical Map of the Counties of Kings and Queens, New York.* New York: W.E. & A.A. Baker, 1859.

Wolverton, Chester. *Atlas of Queens Co., Long Island, New York.* New York: Chester Wolverton, 1891.

The World. 1887–91.

Interviews

Bernstein, John W. Interview by Scott Eckers, August 6, 2020.

Gagarin, Gregory. Interview by Xueyin Zha and Karl D. Qualls. Holy Trinity Russian Orthodox Church Dickinson College, July 3, 2013. http://dh.dickinson.edu/russianamericans/video/holy-trinity-russian-orthodox-church.

Giroffi, Nicholas. Interview by Scott Eckers, regarding the Berg Farmhouse, December 1, 2020.

Hoeffner, Raymond. Interview by Scott Eckers, January 31, 2016.

Kroloff, Charles. Interview by Scott Eckers, regarding Pete Seeger and Community Reform Temple, January 4, 2021.

Kusher, Robert. Interview by Scott Eckers, August 3, 2020.

Labelson, Norman. Interview by Scott Eckers, regarding Salisbury controversy, October 2020.

Manor, Susan. Interview by Scott Eckers, regarding the Temple Sholom History, December 9, 2020.

McVey, George, Jr. Interview by Scott Eckers, April 29, 2022.

Oberle, Joan. Interview by Scott Eckers, February 7, 2016.

Scholl, Burton. Interview by Scott Eckers, regarding school closure debates, July 21, 2022.

Wright, Vincent. Interview by Scott Eckers, May 27, 2021.

INDEX

L

M

ABOUT THE AUTHOR

 uthor, educator and entertainer Dr. Scott M. Eckers is a trustee and past president of the East Meadow Union Free School District. In 2016, he wrote *East Meadow* in Arcadia Publishing's Images of America series and previously helped to establish and curate the Swan Lake Historical Pavilion in the Sullivan County Catskills.

Visit us at
www.historypress.com